LYNNIE,

THANK YOU

MUCH FOR YO[U]

SINCERE FEEDBACK

Phil

This Has All Been Said Before

Phil Hammond

authorHOUSE®

AuthorHouse™
1663 Liberty Drive
Bloomington, IN 47403
www.authorhouse.com
Phone: 1-800-839-8640

First published by AuthorHouse   3/28/2011

ISBN: 978-1-4567-1966-1 (sc)
ISBN: 978-1-4567-1967-8 (hc)
ISBN: 978-1-4567-1968-5 (e)

Library of Congress Control Number: 2011900804

Printed in the United States of America

Author Dedication: To my daughters, Chelsea and Abbygail, you are the constant lights of my life. To my parents, Dwayne and Jean, thank you for everything. To my twin flame. Without you this book could not have been written. With you this book would not have been written. As we were meant, we are. Thank you.

Author's Note

The book you are about to read has purposely been printed only on one side of the page. That this book is an expression of how I perceive truth and life, this should in no way limit the reader to my perceptions. Having read, leant and borrowed too many spiritual and new age books over the past 25 years to have ever kept accurate track of I have consistently filled the books I was reading with notes in the margins, margins that of course never seemed sufficient to the task and rightly so, this was never their intent. Now it is my turn to share and I recognize, perhaps I am beginning to listen to that divine aspect of myself that resides in of all of us, that my truth is only mine and that in the same way that I have come to my understanding you the reader are coming to yours. Any insight I may provide is for you to use to come to discover your own. Truth is of course truth, however we all see it from our own vantage point, through our own eyes. For those readers who are so inclined the blank pages are intended for you to make this book part of your personal search for your truth. If any of what I have to impart reminds you of any aspect of your search, answers any of your questions or is in total disagreement with who you are the space is available for you to record your reactions and thoughts. This is part of my effort to give to others what I would give to myself.

What is the meaning of it, Watson? What is the object of this circle of misery and violence and fear? It must have a purpose or our universe has no meaning, and that is unthinkable. But what purpose? That is humanity's great problem for which reason so far has no answer.

--Sherlock Holmes in The Adventures of the Cardboard Box, by Sir Arthur Conan Doyle.

This Has All Been Said Before

by Phil Hammond

I Give Thanks

From Every Cell of this Body,
With Every Cell of this Body,
To Every Cell of this Body,
I Give Thanks ...

To the Mother Earth and Father Sun.

To the Spirit, Mind, and Body that I Am.

To the four seasons Spring, Summer, Autumn, and Winter.

To the elements of Air, Fire, Metal, Water, and Wood.

To the kingdoms of the Angelic, Microscopic, Vegetation,
Insect, Animal, and Human.

To the Seven Directions: East, South, West, North, Above,
Below, and Beyond.

To the eight additional planets in our solar system, Mercury,
Venus, Mars, Jupiter, Saturn, Uranus, Neptune, and Pluto.

To this solar system, within the Milky Way, within our universe.

Thank you to all of these links in the consciousness of God
that have permitted my creation and my sustenance so that I may
in turn sustain through my creation.
Amen.

Notes

Introduction

Having read **The Occult** by Colin Wilson more than twenty-five years ago, I found my curiosity piqued by the question "Who are we?" Mr. Wilson concluded that the extrasensory powers human beings demonstrated by the acts he chronicled over the better part of two thousand years of our recorded history were the same powers that could save us from ourselves as this world, our world, leaves behind the twentieth century for the twenty-first. He felt—I wonder if he still does—that humanity had only to recognize that we possess these powers in the first place to put us on the path to embracing aspects of ourselves that are much greater than that for which we normally give ourselves credit, and that if we were to do so, we could and would change the course of human history.

At the age of twenty-two, when I read the book that would define my search for the next how many years, I was critical of what humanity was doing to itself, to our environment, and by extension our future on this planet. I wondered if humanity was to Mother Earth what a cancer is to the human body: a part of the living system that completely disregards the system within which it multiplies in an irresponsible and out-of-control fashion, killing not only that which gives it life but itself in the same process. The idea that we possessed an ability to correct the damage we were doing, in my eyes, was very appealing, and I sought out what that power may be. I read alternative-consciousness books, studied spirituality and the martial arts, and tried to come to some understanding of God outside the interpretations provided by our mainstream religions, because they, for whatever reason, were not providing me with any answers that didn't confuse me further and/or raise even more questions than they came close to answering.

I viewed religions as institutions, and my opinion was and remains that an institution always becomes self-serving rather than trying to make itself obsolete because it has accomplished the goals for which it was set up in the first place. I just could not trust what they had to say about who we are and what God's plan is for us. I did,

Notes

however, always believe that despite the self-serving interests of well-intentioned institutions, the truth would be available as long as I just kept searching. I can't tell you why this was so important to me. Kind of like my compulsive habit, I suppose, of always needing to clean a surface of anything that was stuck to it that didn't belong—a compulsion, I might add, that I have done an admirable job keeping just to myself—I needed to peel back the layers of whatever was shielding the truth from me, whatever didn't belong there, with only my conscience as my guide.

Frankly, with or without the help of Mr. Wilson I was on this path regardless. I have always just needed to know "why." Why are we humans polluting our environment to the extent that we are not only killing flora and fauna that are only here to support us in the first place but preventing our home, Mother Earth, from being able to support us? In a society that expects justice to be meted out for the killing of one by another, what sense did it make that we could kill each other by poisoning our environment and nobody seemed to care? "Isn't killing, killing?" I wondered. I had to know why. And what about the extent to which we were using up resources, we being the "developed world," with no regard for the rest of humanity, current and future, who were not permitted the same standard of living our pets enjoyed? This disregard for humanity by humanity just did not make any sense, and then to have to listen to world leaders pay lip service to their concerns about the Third World, especially Third World leaders, was just downright frustrating.

All this time was passing, and I was wrestling with these questions and wondering just what role God was playing in all of this. I was brought up as an atheist, but the more I explored and considered just what creation entailed, the more I came to believe God existed. I still embraced evolution as the process through which life came from simple to more complex forms and interdependencies, but I could no longer believe that life happened as a matter of chance or statistical probability. For me there simply had to be a consciousness that was not necessarily guiding the process we

Notes

see as life but that at least created the parameters within which life could explore itself. However, I was then left questioning what purpose it was serving the Creator to have created life in all of its varied and wonderful and benign forms only to have allowed for the possibility that one life form could come along and mess it up for all the others. What could God possibly have been thinking to allow this to even be a possibility, let alone see it come to fruition? I had to know why.

Well, to my satisfaction I believe I have found the answers to all the questions I had and then some, and I want to share them with anybody who cares to spend some time reading what I have to say. I am not saying that my answers are the only ones—that they are absolute—just that they work for me. By the grace of God I will be able to convey to you the reader how I actually feel about what God is up to, why humanity has followed the path it has, what purpose we as humans, "made in the image of God," are serving in God's plan, and where we may end up. If nothing else my opinions should prove to be provocative and perhaps, just perhaps, illuminating. I may offend, and if I do, I understand how you feel, because I spent much of my life being offended by humanity. With any luck I will provide a remedy for you to deal with this most awful human emotion characterized by self-righteousness, indignation, and victimization. Then again, I may not. Regardless, you will probably come to understand that I take no responsibility for how anybody else feels anyway because I have come to recognize that to do so is only to deny others the opportunity to take responsibility for themselves.

I have come to believe that everything in God's creation has a purpose because life is on purpose. God knew and knows exactly what She or He is up to and has conceived of a plan for life that is absolutely sublime in its design and perfect in its execution. Nothing has been left to chance, and yet every option available is chosen independent of the assistance of God, though within the will of God. God has created a framework within which God cannot lose. By extension neither God nor any aspect of creation

Notes

ever loses, although we are allowed and encouraged to think that we can and do. God hasn't played dice with the universe, but neither does God play chess. Even in a world where perception is 90 percent of reality, there exists an absolute beyond the subjectivity of, let's say, a human point of view. There exists an ultimate reality from which we came and to which we are going back that, by the way, isn't any more or less important to the grand scheme of things than any other aspect of subjective creation. In God's eyes, "everything is beautiful, in its own way."

Notes

God, Source, Creator, Allah, Brahman

For those who believe, no explanation is necessary.
For those who do not, no explanation will do.
    Anonymous

That there exists a consciousness from which the physical laws of nature emanate, that created all of the known and unknown universe, including our world, as well as having devised and implemented the plan through which life would be expressed, to me is self-evident. I look at all of our world and the universe we have access to and I wonder, "How could all of this have spontaneously appeared?" Frankly—and though I do not mean to offend, I am aware I very well may—I wonder if people who reject the notion of God aren't just as blind as those who accept that the world was literally created in seven days, and yet I try to embrace that these perspectives, too, serve their purpose. The only way that anything man has created can exist is because there was man to create it. How could what is infinitely more complex and mysterious than anything man could ever conceive, namely the universe, come into being by itself? Of course I have my own theory about why people reject the notion of a Creator, but my speculations are moot. Just the fact that they do is all that matters, and I hope to explain that they are just as important an aspect of God's plan as every other human thought, word, and deed, as I describe what kind of a God makes sense to me. Oh, and by the way, to you nonbelievers, God does not need your permission to exist, just as the earth did not need the support of the church to be a sphere. What exists does so regardless.

To me God is simply the sum consciousness of all the energy in the universe. God is everything, and that I cannot put into words what is beyond words is not much of an issue for me. God knows that I am aware of Her being aware of me and all of creation, and we are good with that. Taoist writings describe that which cannot be described, that which has no beginning and no end, that to which we can aspire but never know. In even trying to describe God we have only words, which are limited in that they can only represent,

1

Notes

yet are being used to describe, that which is limitless—a taller order than I will even attempt. Still, I am comfortable with my previous definition that God is the sum consciousness of all the energy in the universe. From this perspective God has Her complete attention on all of creation, every singular aspect in every single moment, because all of creation is God. Everything is but an expression of energy, and in saying it is only energy I mean that it is everything. Energy is everything because everything is energy. Because all of creation is God, there cannot be one aspect of creation that does not serve a purpose or have a reason for existing. Why would God waste any aspect of Her self when God has complete control over the expression of Her self? Again to me this is self-evident, and that there are those who disagree is certain. However, they of course can only do so from my perspective, because He created and allowed for this circumstance and possibility to be. The very fact that we don't all share the same point of view, that we could see and support different perspectives, is only, in my opinion, because God created the possibility of every different human perspective in the first place. Perspectives may contradict each other, but that doesn't mean they eliminate each other. God knows humans have and continue to attempt this, but now that I think about it, that is only because God created this possibility too.

So if God is Creator—which I believe God is, and you are certainly invited to agree or disagree—if God is all energy, all consciousness, then creation must be inclusive. Everything must be included, because nothing can exist outside of God's intent; everything is an expression of energy. It follows, then, that if all is God, there can be no accidents or coincidence, for everything has a reason. What we don't understand and might consider a fluke, an accident, a coincidence, or a statistical anomaly does in fact not fall outside the preserve of God. Rather it represents an opportunity for our understanding of what life is to expand. The interesting part is that there are those who believe that there are expressions that exist outside of God, to counter, object, and conflict with God—Satan, for example. Again in my worldview these ideas can exist only because God created the possibility, and in coming to

Notes

understand the purpose that such an oppositional belief fulfills, we will only come that much closer to understanding God. I believe that everything, all knowledge, will be ours when we are ready and that for now what suits my purpose is not being able to describe what God is so much as what God is up to. Why? I want to know what motivated God to create this world and to create us. I want to know how our human experience serves that purpose, because there has to be one, since everything has a purpose.

And God created man in His own image, in the image of God He created him; male and female He created them. Genesis 1:27

I always found the idea that God created humanity in Her image compelling, though I was never comfortable with the idea that we literally, physically were created in Her image. To me, God, being limitless as an image is everything we see, experience, and can imagine. Is there anything that God is not? God is the sum consciousness of all the energy in the universe, so if something exists, it does so not just by the grace of God but as an expression of God. The animist philosophies of our planet that see God in everything make the most sense to me, but still, what is meant in the book of Genesis where it says God made man in Her image? This question always stayed with me, and then I read **Conversations with God, Book One**, by Neale Donald Walsch. I was given my answer, in part. In this book God discusses with the author what motivated Him to create, and the answer is as profound as it is simple: for the sake of knowledge. God describes how over a period of time beyond our imagination She existed conceptually aware of everything that God is. As pure energy, this ability to conceive and explore of course knew no bounds because the awareness was and is limitless. However, God came to realize that Her knowledge of who she is was only partially available to Her in Her pure energy form, and that the rest of the knowledge that would complete Her understanding would be available to Her only through experience. Imagine that you could see a picture of a strawberry, hold a strawberry in your hand, and have somebody

Notes

describe to you what a strawberry tastes like. Until you actually get to taste a strawberry (preferably my mom's strawberries with whipped cream atop her sweet biscuits) your knowledge of what a strawberry is and what it tastes like would be incomplete. God created to experience and thereby complete Her knowledge.

But how then were we created in God's image? We learn the same way God does, through experience and only by experiencing. We weren't created physically in God's image; we were created intellectually in God's image. How many times have you heard someone described as "having to learn the hard way." Well, if you choose, you can blame this seeming malady on God. We are curious creatures because we have to be. We can't just take somebody else's word for everything, we have to try it for ourselves, and depending upon who we are and how far away we feel from Source, the limits to which we will listen or not are decided. Some people have less curiosity than others, some people forfeit their lives because of it, and yet others take another's word and avoid just about anything. Regardless, the rule remains the same: we gain complete knowledge only through direct experience, the same as God.

Hold on, though. I just mentioned "direct experience," but how can God be having direct experience if Her creation is the one having the experience? I previously mentioned the animist perspective of God, that God is in everything because everything is God. Does that mean, by extension, that we humans are God? In a sense I believe it does, though I want to point out that we are singular perspectives of God, limited by our experience and the knowledge we have yet to acquire. But yes, in a sense we are God, just as in a sense we are not. As a physical body that certainly is finite we are not all that God is, and we don't have to be. As an expression of our soul—that aspect of ourselves that is in complete contact with who we are and that from which we came—we are infinite and forever and God. We are truly amazing creatures being used by God, to co-create with God to realize everything God is and isn't, which by the way contributes to everything that God is.

7

Notes

But for God to truly experience who and what God is, from the human perspective, God had to overcome a stumbling block created by the need to experience everything God is not as well. Let me explain. Our physical universe is relative; that is, nothing can exist except in relation to something else. I think this is what Einstein was referring to when he came up with his theory of relativity, but I could be mistaken. For example, if everything was at a constant temperature (pick any number), temperature would not exist. There would be a constant, but with nothing to compare it with, that temperature would have no meaning. Of course it would exist, but the idea of temperature would be of no consequence. Introduce different temperatures, though, and what used to be the constant temperature, because of different temperatures can now either be appreciated or not. At least it will have significance; it will matter. The more that different temperatures are experienced, the more the knowledge of temperature becomes complete. Trust me: I am from Canada, and immigrants from the tropics experiencing their first Canadian winter appreciate their tropical homes much differently when they have to brave a minus 20-degree centigrade day, let alone something in the minus 30-degree range. This is what experience gives us: knowledge, perspective, and appreciation. This is what God gets from us: the perspective of appreciation for having created a physical world and aspects of God that can explore the duality and relativity of that world.

Once something is known, it is known. Though we can forget, being reminded never brings the same sensation of discovery as learning it for the first time. God, who has conceived of everything and created everything and therefore to an extent is aware of everything, cannot not know what is known. As the saying goes, once the toothpaste is out of the tube, it is not going back in. How then can God experience learning anything and experience excitement from having discovered? This is where we humans come in. God created human beings having forgotten who human being are, creative partners of God and with God, thus serving two purposes: it makes it fun for God, and it makes it fun for us! Really it does. Only by beginning our journey, the process called

Notes

life, and not remembering who we are is it guaranteed that we will explore all aspects of who we are not. Who we are not falls under the general category of fear, which, negatively expressed, is everything that love is not. If we were created remembering who we are, like a mammal born under water we would just head right for the surface back to God and really have not fulfilled any purpose of discovery, experience, or contribution to knowledge. However, we are created having forgotten, so when we do discover a truth, it truly seems like a discovery for having not been aware of the truth in the first place. With no challenge there can be no triumph, and not remembering who we are is a challenge. It can be painful, and yes, there can appear to be suffering, but all of this is necessary if there is to be perspective and appreciation and knowledge, for both us and God. Keep in mind, God cannot not know, but God can experience firsthand what it is like to come to a place of knowing from not knowing, learning, if we genuinely seem to, if it is real to us, and the perception is all that is required to make it real for us and by extension for God. God is living and learning and growing vicariously through creation, through God, and all that is really real is the knowledge God is gaining from the experience. Everything else is perspective.

Perspective then is everything, which is why it is also necessary for the experience of "what is" to be complemented by the experience of "what is not." Just as temperature could not exist were it not for different temperatures, neither is emotion complete without experiencing what love is and what love is not, and these experiences have to be real to us for them to matter. Even though ultimately all there is, is love, we have to live, breathe, and believe in fear. Fear in all of its forms must be experienced, expressed, and yes, feared to make emotion real. The fear of loss, the fear of death, the fear of hunger and loneliness, and even the fear of being who we are, God, are necessary. If they didn't hurt and produce suffering, they would not be real. They would not matter, and neither would the times when we were not having to experience them and were experiencing abundance and love and joy instead. This is what God has done for God's self and this is who we are,

Notes

playing our role in the game. Make no mistake, this is a game when you are ready to see it that way. Perspective truly is a magical aspect of life and like all magic can be controlled when understood. Perspective can and will be greatly accepted and appreciated from this understanding, but this comes only from not knowing it and rejecting it because "its" discovery becomes real for us, even though it has always been there.

What then makes perspective real, our point of view matter? From the Buddhist perspective two things in life are constant—and no, they are not death and taxes. Instead the two tenets are that life is difficult and that everything changes. What I have come to understand, however, is that life always changes because life is difficult, and if it were not for the changes, then life would not and could not exist. Creation has to evolve in order to matter. Just as a moment exists only because there is something to compare the present moment with, the past and the future, and just as temperature and emotions exist because they can and do change, experience and the knowledge it produces for us and God can exist only because it too changes. It moves, revolves, and evolves. This movement is critical and necessary regardless of how much we humans try to keep everything the same. Interestingly enough, the more we try to keep them the same, the more we are only ensuring they will change, just not as we would like, which is of course part of the process as well, because everything is. Change is not just inevitable, it is all there is. Life cannot help changing any more than water can help being wet and the sky can only be blue, except when it isn't. Life is not about change—life is change. This is a constant, and it is a constant that moves from the simple to the complicated, from the basic to the profound, and everything as an aspect of life contributes in its own way to life, to change.

This is why I see God and all of creation as being inclusive. If God has the power, and the means with which to create everything (and yes, I am simply going to ignore the possibility that God does not), there can't be "mistakes, misfits or accidents, just humans not understanding," according to Black Swan in Marlo

13

Notes

Morgan's, **Mutant Message Down Under.** Even the realities that humans do not understand, or that we don't believe in God, or that we do not conceive completely of who and what God is, exist as possibilities and realities only because God created them as possibilities in the first place and they serve a purpose. They provide for balance, for duality, without which their reflection could not exist. How many religions believe that there is only one way to God, their way? How many people believe there is only one way to live a life, their way? How many people, based upon their perspective, would deny another person the right to find their own way? Maybe not you, the reader, maybe not us personally—I know I have never judged another person from my own limited perspective—but generally speaking it seems to be quite the norm for humanity to look at life in terms of exclusivity: that there is right at the exclusion of that which is wrong, there is up at the exclusion of that which is down, there is God at the exclusion of that which is Satan—or maybe there is Satan at the exclusion of God! I know this is experienced as being real; we live it and teach it to our children and separate ourselves from each other and sit justified in killing each other only because we can exclude another from who we think we are. But this exclusive attitude is with us only because God created and allowed and accepts it in all of its forms because it fulfills a purpose, and that purpose is perspective, knowledge, and change. Imagine: even thinking we are separate from God or creation or each other is only a part of the experience we call life. And who says that God doesn't have a sense of humor?

God is in complete control of His creation, and part of that control is us believing that He is not. Amazing. We are moving through our lives, worrying and fearing, loving and enjoying, providing God with a singular perspective toward life, our personal perspective that will never be duplicated. We act so unGod-like at times and so God-like at others, reacting to circumstances and effects that we have created on some level, playing, so to speak, in God's backyard at a game that we may not even know exists. Everything is happening for a reason because there is a reason for everything. All the death, all the pain, all the suffering

Notes

matters, not because it is ultimately real but because it provides for perspective, knowledge, and change. We are life and we are change, and the only relief—real relief—in sight is our coming to this understanding and then being able to accept and allow. This is where God resides, in acceptance and allowance. God sees, completely, how every aspect of creation serves to complement all of creation, and regardless of the feeling that is evoked by any circumstance the benefit of that experience outweighs the cost of not being able to have it. Remember, God existed forever not having experience, and now that God is having experience, from a perspective of allowance and acceptance God loves it all. As we change and live and grow, we move toward this perspective to who we are, and everything changes with us. This is life and this is who we are, and rejecting it all is only a part of—a necessary part of—coming to embrace that we accept it all, just as God does.

Circle of Life

Source:
God-Brahman-Allah-Spirit-Divine
(As You Wish)

Unconscious Creation		Conscious Creation

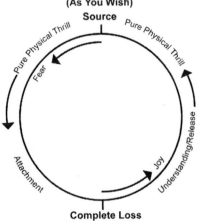

Unconscious Creation

Selfish-Unselfishness

Manipulation, Control

Right Vs. Wrong

Living Without

Rejection

Judgement

Seperation, Individual

Distrustful, Unhappy

Fear-Anger-Anxiety

Limitation Deception

Darkness

Absolute

Conscious Creation

Unselfish-Selfishness

Allowance

Working/Not Working

Living Within

Accomodation

Acceptance

Fellowship, One of All

Confidence-Joy-Calm

Freedom-Truth-Love

Honesty, Release

Light

Subjective

Source

Pure Physical Thrill

Pure Physical Thrill

Fear

Understanding/Release

Attachment

Joy

Complete Loss

The Circle of Life

proc·ess
a continuous action, operation, or series of changes
taking place in a definite manner: *the process of life.*

I see life as a process, that is, I see God as a process, as God
expresses and is expressed. There is nothing within this process
that can exist outside the realm of creation. The process is
inclusive. It includes everything that can be experienced and
manifested, excluding nothing, including the idea that there are
aspects of creation beyond the control of God. Believing that
we can subvert the will of God is only another aspect of God's
allowance. God has a plan and through creation is allowing that
plan to unfold, to grow, and in turn to re-create God. This plan is
indeed a process. There is a definite and continuous action that is
taking place of which we and all creation are a part, represent, and
contribute to. The process does not necessarily lead us anywhere,
though it does allow for change and growth. This can be hard to
see and understand, but in the difficulty of this understanding lies
the opportunity for the excitement of discovery. The process of
life, the circle of life, is the means through which life is expressed
and explored. This is all done for its own sake, making it the reason
and the purpose, the means and the end, the alpha and the omega.
Life is experiencing itself just for the sake of being able to, and
for the same reason, experiencing, life must change so experience
can exist at all. Without different experience to compare itself
with, experience stops. In the absence of different experience,
experience ceases to have meaning. Life exists in the first place
because in its absence there is only awareness, no complete
knowledge, no challenge, no triumph, no death, no birth, no fear,
and no love expressed, just awareness—but no fun.

Because the process is the means and the end, the vehicle through
which God arrives at Himself, a circle represents metaphorically
and beautifully the process of life. Every point on a circle can
represent a human perspective; every point is necessary to

Notes

contribute to the strength that is the circle and to maintain the integrity that is the circle. And all points lead back to themselves, after having experienced all the other points of view. Individually we are each our own circle. Collectively we contribute to the greater circle that is all experience that is God. Our personal circle, which really is not personal as much as it is soulful, traces our path as we leave God and begin to make our way back to God, each and every step along the way, in every life that we live throughout this process, represented, accounted for, as a link in a chain, all necessary to make that chain whole, to keep the experience intact. Each step is a balancing act, reflecting and representing the emotion from which it was motivated, conceived, and created, either moving into the universe as cause or coming back from creation to us as effect.

Referred to as karma in some traditions, this is the cosmic balancing act through which energy maintains balance or is seeking balance, and the circle is the testament to the veracity of this process. We move away from God, increasingly directed by fear, as God intended. The farther we move from Source, the more our actions and their effects push us away from God. The effects I am referring to, of course, are pain and suffering. By design they cause us more pain and suffering, and we are continually processing ourselves, creating imbalance from our fear. It has to come back to us not unlike a cosmic debt that we will pay back through having to experience that which we have created. Pain and suffering are not a punishment but simply an effect we have delivered upon ourselves unconsciously. That is how we are living as we leave God, unconsciously, on that side of the circle where we are moving away from Source, leading to that point opposite and farthest away from Source. We were created forgetting who we are so we would purposely explore all those aspects of who we are not, and this is fear. This reality fulfills the duality that is a relative existence. If this were not the case, if we remembered who we were from the start, we would simply make our way directly back, denying ourselves the experience of "discovering" ourselves, for we would never have felt lost. Only by feeling 'lost' can God

Mountain That Is
Human Experience

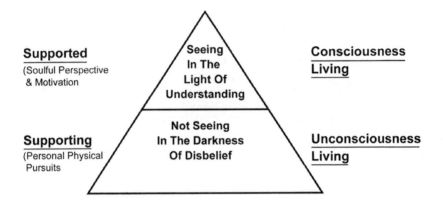

be provided the experience and therefore the perspective and appreciation by us, God's children, for having lived and explored everything God is not.

I find—and perhaps this is an appropriate juncture at which to introduce the metaphor of the mountain—that the circle cannot necessarily tell the whole story. I love the idea of a mountain representing the sum of human experience as well as each individual soul's complete experience. I appreciate the mountain because it takes us into a third dimension that allows for the idea of being able to see farther the higher we move up its sides, mirroring how we as humans start to see more of who we are and what the process is that we are a part of and in fact represent as we gain experience. The bottom of the mountain represents that first half of the circle where decisions are motivated by fear, made in the myopic state where, metaphorically, because of the trees and low altitude, our ability to see very far at all is obscured to say the least. We see very little of others, we see very little of the mountain, we see very little of anything except ourselves and conduct ourselves accordingly. Self-preservation is the order of the day, and in all of its various forms we act like the animals we are not, in the absence of the greater understanding that we are moving toward. Gradually, consistently, and unerringly, though, despite any feeling to the contrary, we are moving through the trees, climbing higher, retracing our routes on occasion as we discover choices that lead only to dead ends, muddying our boots on other occasions and scraping our knees or bloodying ourselves on yet others.

Despite all the trials and tribulations we do move higher, and as we do, we start to make a connection between our actions and our experience. We begin to understand that as we treat others we are only treating ourselves, because the reactions we experience and the imbalance of energy that we create and then have visited upon ourselves becomes undeniable from the evidence in front of us. Recognizing that we are the source of everything we have experienced is akin to having started to reach the tree line on our mountain. The mountain, the sky, and the surrounding vista

23

Notes

becomes available to us, and we can finally recognize from the light of understanding now shining upon us that we are one, that all is necessary to understand this, that we were never lost, and that it is the process, the process of change marked by every step along the way, that is responsible. The only way we can reach that point of seeing, and the next and the next, we come to recognize, is through every step we ever took where we could not see. As we come to accept that we are not less for having taken them, we also see that in others, because now we can.

Now we begin moving up our mountain, and higher truths become available to us the higher we climb, because we can see farther and more of the mountain becomes available for us to see—not because there was any place to get to, mind you, but because of the experience we were having in each and every moment along the way. We begin to understand that not only are we responsible for all of our choices and their consequences but only we personally can be responsible. We had the authority and the power in the first place, and we can have this power only because all of humanity does. Life does not happen to us, we happen to life. We are not a part of the process as much as we are the process. We are co-creative partners with God, because we are singular complete reflections of God, providing for God and ourselves and the universe a perspective of living that has never been provided before and will never be provided again. We have thus begun to love ourselves as we come to know ourselves.

Judgment and rejection that characterized the view we had of ourselves and the world around us no longer can hold sway. Acceptance and allowance begin to dominate our worldview as the altitude of our being comes to see how every step along the way matters. Imagine being a good way up a mountain, far enough up that the bottom is now visible to a large extent. Now as you are looking, enjoying the view your climb has afforded you, an idea comes to you, something so simple yet profound that your view of the mountain changes. For whatever reason, you, we, come to understand that the top portion of the mountain can only be the

25

Notes

top for the support provided by the bottom. Only through the work we did coming up from the bottom of the mountain—work that admittedly wasn't always fun—could we have gotten to that place where the reward of the view made it all worthwhile. We also begin to notice that even though our path and the paths of others were very different along the way, the higher we move the more we come together. Could this be the promise of truth? We begin to embrace, because of the truth now afforded, the fact that we owe our awakening to our past ignorance, our previous steps. We have nothing to apologize for, ever, and we especially expect no apologies from others, though we will gladly accept them if this is anybody else's wish, because we recognize that whatever we have given to others we have given only to ourselves. To give another understanding through the acceptance of their now unnecessary apology is to love ourselves as we love them. We see that giving to others without expectation is only giving to ourselves and truly controlling through allowance the experience we wish to have. We are being unselfishly selfish*, because we know that giving love is receiving love, and we have enough experience of giving ourselves the effects of fear to have learned better, our knowledge having become that complete.

*Unselfishly selfish is the recognition that only by taking care of ourselves first can we hope to take care of others. What appears to be selfish by those who would instead be acting selfishly unselfish is instead anything but. Unselfishly selfish is thought in action that we are one, that individually we can and must take care of ourselves and give ourselves value first if we are to be of productive value to another. Leading by example that we are the creative authority in process allows others to see this for themselves and become the independent contributing humans we all are. Selfish unselfishness on the other hand represents having not yet made the connection with who we are. Believing that we justify ourselves through the praise or acceptance we can only get from others, what we do for others is not our primary motive rather it is for the recognition we believe we should receive for doing whatever we have done. What appears to be unselfish is actually very selfish and has at its root fear. God does a wonderful job, as only Allah can, in describing this condition in the Conversations with God series.

Notes

We also come to recognize that to "feel" the presence of God, we only have to move to that place where God is—to acceptance and allowance—and this all comes naturally; it is the only way it can. We have learned that forcing an issue will never work, because in the very act of forcing anything, who we are being and who we are saying to the universe we are is somebody who is without; therefore we need to seek and try in the first place. Moving up the proverbial mountain shows us that our thoughts and beliefs are the creative basis of what we have received and what we will perceive. Thus in the process of believing we are "without," our being is created by ourselves and supported by the universe. Our lives and our experience both reflect and support truth through revealing that we designed the circumstances that delivered any pain and suffering into our lives. Now, from higher upon the mountain, we use this understanding of who we are to create love and joy, by giving this to others, as an expression of having it to give. As we do, we are acting like God and begin to move into God, consciously, aware that to "feel" God is only to have finally come to that place energetically where God is. God has always been with us, we recognize, but we could feel at one with God only when we came to realize that we are. Again, the truth that thoughts and beliefs define experience and reality is supported. By loving ourselves, as God does, unconditionally and completely, for having come to that place of acceptance through understanding and knowledge guaranteed by experience, we allow ourselves this new perspective. This is what is waiting for us as human beings, but again—and it deserves to recognized at every turn—this place with God, like every other point in experience, is not the reason or purpose for creation. Rather it is one more necessary aspect of the process that is creation that has no destination because there is no beginning and no end to **everything!**

I wonder—and seeing as this is my book, I can—if many religious traditions are lost on this subject of process and lack of destination. Abstinence seems to be a common form of religious expression, as if going "without" will bring us closer to God, or even as if being "closer to God" is better than being where we are, feeling as if we

Notes

are not close to God. I feel that what religions and beliefs that reflect this type of thinking are in fact promoting and encouraging is to be putting the proverbial cart before the horse in their attempt to find union with God for having confused cause and effect. Those teachers who came before, who want for nothing, did not come to where they are because they abstained. Rather they want for nothing as a reflection of how close they have come to God, and they were able to come close to God only because they learned what they did from not abstaining in the first place. We don't have to go without to move closer to God as much as we only have to go within. Denying ourselves, as another expression of sponsoring thought, only supports feeling separate from God because our belief is that we are, and therefore we have to do something to remedy the situation. Doing supports our being and continues to do so until we understand the strength of being, at which time doing becomes a conscious reflection of awareness of being. Being is the dog and doing is the tail, always. When we have figured this out, we will have also come to that place where the acceptance of all experience as necessary is recognized. Not worrying about anything, especially our proximity to God, as the expression of our "being" allows us to be one with everything, especially God, without doing a darn thing and doing through allowance instead of doing from rejection. Yet again we are all coming to recognize that there is no place to be and are doing so by trying to get there. This is all a part of the process and all we do supports the process that after all is the purpose of life.

Accepting that there has never been a destination, though the top of the mountain might suggest otherwise, that life is a circle spiraling in on itself, so to speak, growing and changing, is to be in the moment. Appreciating where we are, with no concern for the past because the past has been accepted as the only means through which lessons could be learned, and not worrying for the future, for it is understood that everything can be fine only because it always is, is to release ourselves into the infinite creative possibility in each moment. Without the distraction of "before" or "after" we allow ourselves to "be" and the possibilities of our

Notes

potential become available to us. Still, even coming to this place is but a phase we will go through, only another step along the path of life, a life without destination, only discovery. How much farther there is to go, I have yet to know. In fact I am still in the process of shedding my old habits and understanding, and I spend very little time in the moment even though I have glimpsed it. However, I will continue to see more and more of the bigger picture as I process, just as we all do. I may not see it all, but I know it is there, and I know it will be revealed to me because it will be revealed to us all when we are ready, as part of our lightening up. This is God, acceptance and allowance, and as we move into this place, we find what we have always been. God does not play dice with the universe, as Mr. Einstein so duly noted. Einstein maintained that everything observable in nature was and is a perfect balancing act working in harmony with itself in a manner that defies imagination and explanation. Because of this perfection, because God has not taken any chances, God does not have to play chess with His creation. She knows, as we all will come to know, that the process is self-actualizing and is displaying its potential as it fulfills its purpose, to discover itself. From this perfection allowance permits the discovery to be realized and enjoyed. Everything is fine. God knows this, and we are only coming to remember it ourselves as both a part of the process and being the process itself.

Notes

Free Will/Choice

In a life that is on purpose, where everything happens for a reason—because there is a reason for everything—can there truly exist free choice or free will? If no human thought, word, or deed can exist outside the scope of creation, if our Creator has provided for all, and therefore life is completely and entirely inclusive, no human choice can be made that exists outside the realm of Allah. If no choice can be made that is not already on the menu, are we ultimately choosing anything? If this is the case, which only makes sense to me, then how free could our choices ever be? How free is our will? Perhaps it is free in the sense that God does not personally judge us or punish us for choices we have made, though some religions would have us believe otherwise, in which case it strikes me that from their perspective, "free choice" is much more clearly defined as "conditional choice," that is, decision making comes with conditions that determine whether a person will be allowed into heaven. From my perspective, however, where not a single one of us will ever be denied entrance "back home" by God or ourselves, what difference do our choices make if our destiny is to explore all that creation is, which includes everything that God is not? If we cannot consider anything that has not been allowed for, said, or done except that which lies within the realm of creation, free will is certainly not ours to control separately from anything, because everything is the will of God.

Ultimately, absolutely, we do not exercise free choice, free will, or control over our lives, because all aspects of all lives are but a reflection of God's will, except—and this might be the kicker—subjectively, when from a personal perspective it is important to us that we believe otherwise. I have heard it said that the greatest expression of our free will is to have chosen to give our will to the will of God. This for me begs the question and underlies my assertion that we do not have free will, ultimately, to give. In a process of inclusion where everything exists only as an expression

35

Notes

of God and God's conception of reality, how can we ever not be living the will of God? Obviously "feeling" that we are not living the will of God serves a purpose; that we could oppose God and have "free choice" to do so is important. This feeling of being able to deny God is necessary, of course, if we are to fully appreciate discovering that we have always been fulfilling God's desire. I would contend, therefore, that the greatest expression of our free will is in our discovering that we have always lived the will of God and as such have no reason to carry regret for anything and in finding this grace in ourselves we can now share this with humanity.

Until such time, free choice—at least the feeling that we have and exercise free choice—belongs to the preserve of a reasoning that sees ourselves as separate, and our motives and beliefs, to a very large extent reflect this perspective of fear. Fear, as one of its many facets, produces a feeling of needing to be in control as a means to avoid something from going "wrong" in one's life. This feeling of needing to avoid, to minimize the opportunity for pain and suffering to come into our lives, I believe, is a product of our subconsciously knowing that separately we are vulnerable. We believe we are separate and vulnerable; hence the need to feel as if we are in control. We hold on to the idea of free choice as a drowning man grabs a sword, because we see it as a means to control things in a life that is out of control because of being separate.

Free choice/will is also used as a foundation to support the idea of judgment and the belief in right versus wrong that characterizes living on the unconscious side of the circle of life. Without the idea of free choice, how could we ever hold anybody responsible for actions we deem contrary to the benefit of society or give adulation and reward to those who seemingly exceed the contributions of an average human? Good versus bad, right versus wrong, happy versus sad: all these conditions and more can exist only if we accept as truth that choices we make either support or run contrary to the workings of our own lives and that of God. Judgment based upon our own definitions, as reflections of our

Notes

beliefs, can exist only if there is something to reject in the first place. Believing in free choice allows for rejection, allows for us to have a world within which the decisions we make can be judged by others and judged by ourselves. Free choice is a necessary pillar to support humanity's current understanding, without which most of our society and our view of human history would crumble. Clearly we are not ready for our current understanding to change by this magnitude, but it is coming.

Having yet to fully remember who we are collectively, humanity clings to the idea of free choice, just as we are supposed to. If we were created fully remembering who we are—that is, complete, whole, and holy—we would have no need to explore the effects of rejection, separateness, and all expressions of fear because we would simply accept life, all of life, as necessary whether we currently see the relevance or not. By not exploring completely who we are not, exemplified by rejection through the idea of free choice, we would be denying God and ourselves a perspective of knowledge available only when both sides of love, love and fear, are experienced. Without cold and hot there is no appreciation, and therefore complete knowledge, of temperature. Without exploring everything that we are not, rejection, we would have no sense of accomplishment in finding who we really are, acceptance, because there would have not been the experience of a challenge. In a relative world where something, anything, can completely exist only in relation to its other side, experiencing both sides is imperative, and the idea of free choice allows us to explore rejection and allowance, even though ultimately it does not exist because there is only God's choice.

In not remembering who we are and in feeling separate from ourselves, each other, and our Creator, we make choices that allow us to explore every facet, every angle of creation, primarily from the perspective of fear. In trying to not make mistakes, as if we could do anything wrong, we attempt to control by minimizing pain and maximizing pleasure in our lives. We do this of course with the best of intentions to take care of ourselves, using our

Notes

"free choice," all the while creating ripples of karmic energy that come back to us as a perfect reflection of the energy we expended in the first place. As we experience these "ripples," we come to recognize the ramifications of our choices, the direct link between us as the cause and the effect. If our primary motive is fear, the universe will give it back to us, not as a punishment but in support of our being. When we can no longer ignore the responsibility we have for the creation of our experience, because of the energy reflection we see before and around our lives in the circumstances we come to endure, we are well on our way to remembering who we are. We are all creative, all powerful, singular aspects of the One.

To fully appreciate, however, that we have only ever been fulfilling the will of God, in fact leading sacred lives, we must believe, act, and create as if we are not. Thinking we are exercising free will supports this aspect of learning. Even though we cannot ultimately exercise choice separate from creation, we have to believe, for some time, that we are doing just that, and that the possibility has been provided for us for itself, by Source. Our hearts, that physical connection we have with our soul and thereby, Brahman, really are controlling all aspects of our lives. Our souls "see" the big picture and know the experience we, personally, need to have to contribute to completing themselves and their work through us to achieve this end. Our souls use us through our hearts and, within the illusion of fear, our heads, the physical aspect of ourselves that is the home to our separate individual reality. Our heads are allowed, through reason and logic, to have and maintain beliefs of fear and separateness and from these beliefs make all decisions, decisions that ultimately could lead to our deaths or the deaths of others. Just as Jesus "allowed" himself to be crucified so that he could show us that we cannot be killed, that we are **"forever people,"** through His resurrection, our hearts allow our heads to make the same choices for the same end, sacrificing the body so knowledge can be imparted. Our heads have to have the illusion that they are doing this to themselves of their own free will for the knowledge to be complete so that reason can discover

Notes

on its own that life is but a reflection of perspective, that we have been exercising the power that we are all along, and that this power is consciously of service to us when we have learned to direct it inwardly, to controlling ourselves, instead of outwardly, trying to control others' thus the purpose of the illusion of free will is exposed. We have to know that we are hurting ourselves to learn how to not hurt ourselves. Making choices from a defensive, protective, and fearful perspective will produce this same experience. In effect we are controlling our experience, except the outcome was never in doubt, which of course is contrary to the belief that delivered us there. Doubt leads to confidence just as fear leads to love. Ignorance is but a necessary step to knowledge.

How many times have I heard that emotional stress is the number one cause of physical death? Too many times to have kept track, I am sure. A body that is overloaded with worry, one that is always attempting to control everything around it that it possibly can for fear that something might go wrong if it does not "do all that it could," does so because it believes that life is wrong or could go wrong. Physiologically the flight-or-fight response is constantly in operation, the adrenal system on constant alert at the expense of the immune and digestive systems. Sooner or later disease claims a life as a symptom of the problem, thinking, and beliefs that do not support life.

Jesus' teachings about reincarnation have been found. We live many lives concurrently, experienced as past and future lives, and in most of them the above scenario is the common denominator. The impression of free choice comes with a feeling of responsibility. When we finally get "It," we do so because we know that anything we have ever experienced we have created ourselves, all of it. An alcoholic will seek to help himself only after he admits he has a problem, and that same alcoholic will be successful in dealing with his addiction only when he discovers that the source of his problem is himself. In that case, the idea of free choice and free will has done its job. By learning through experience what works for having explored everything that does not work, we conclude

Notes

that there was never anything to worry about, especially whether we had control or not through the possession of free will, because our safety was never in jeopardy in the first place. We cannot be lost, we cannot be killed, we cannot ever be without; life can only seem this way. As William Shakespeare, truly a prophet of God from my perspective, so eloquently said, "It is neither good nor bad, but thinking makes it so."

Our destination, even though there is not one, is guaranteed; only how we get there will be individual. Just as creation allows us to come to this understanding so that all the paths and possibilities of creation will be exorcised along the way and thus knowledge made complete, the heart allows the head to come to understand that not only is it not in control but it no longer has to try to be, because it recognizes that it never was. Once the head realizes that it is not in control, that the idea of free choice is but an illusion, it is prepared to give up the beliefs—any and all beliefs—it once held about who it is and what life is about. The flight-or-fight approach to life can be allowed to transform into acceptance and allowance because it is realized that if there ever was a threat, it came only from within. Even more important, however, the insight that is gained is that indulging the illusion of flight or fight in the first place was necessary but no longer is because it provided the knowledge from which life could grow and change.

Free will, or the feeling of free will, provides the same perspective. Once we realize that we have only been living the will of God, and will only ever live the will of God, can we then truly begin consciously creating our destiny, because we will be coming to life from a perspective of love rather than the alternative, fear. True creation has very little to do with doing, compared with being. In allowing ourselves the gift of knowing that everything is fine, that it always has been and always will be, we are being thankfulness in the process. This is the domain of God and is truly appreciated for ever having seemed otherwise. This is why God has given us and Her/Himself the illusion of darkness, the deception of free choice, so that complete knowledge could be appreciated. And so it is.

Notes

Pain and Suffering

In our sleep, pain which cannot forget falls, drop by drop, upon the heart until in our despair, against our will, comes wisdom through the awful grace of God.
Aeschylus

Pain, at least what we perceive as pain, both emotional and physical, is the fuel that runs the engine that moves us through the circle of life. Were it not for the experience of pain we would never explore the metaphorical mountain of human experience to its full extent; we would never move from that place of not remembering who we are to complete realization. Pain and the suffering it creates provides the incentive to grow beyond. Pain is not something to be avoided, necessarily. Rather it comes to be celebrated, because it not only protects us until we get to a place where we can put it into perspective but provides the means by which we get to that place. Pain is seen as a necessary evil of sorts and like all of this reality is totally subjective, even though ultimately it is a portal to universal truth.

Every human choice, word, thought, and action is supported by how we feel we can best minimize pain and maximize pleasure. The foundation from which we make these choices are our beliefs, beliefs that can be conscious or unconscious. Our beliefs are a reflection of where we are on our path. It can also be said that our elevation on the mountain of experience is determined by our beliefs. Whichever way we choose to look at it, the choices we make reflect who we think we are. Do we think we are separate from ourselves, each other, God, our Mother Earth? Do we believe there is not enough, and that we have to get as much as possible? Do we believe in fear and try to do everything we can to minimize all that could potentially go wrong around us? This type of thinking, although not wrong, represents being lower on the mountain or the unconscious side of the circle of life and produces results very different from being higher on the mountain. These effects, of which we are the cause, protect us by giving us the opportunity to see how we create the reality we live in, and

Notes

from this we learn to make different choices to produce different results. We grow.

Energy is always either in balance or seeking balance. We, as co-creators of reality, affect energy, the energy of the universe, the energy that is God. Our thoughts, manifested as words and actions, create energy ripple effects that can and will always be directly experienced as they come back to their source seeking balance. Negative thoughts and actions, those produced from a generally defensive position, are experienced for what they are, negative perceptions. Take a look at what we as humans are doing to our planet's ecology. That which supports us is literally being ruined because of human fear-based motives expressed and justified through the pursuit of progress, as if progress holds the key to human security and happiness. This used to concern me, but it doesn't any longer. There have been five major extinctions throughout the history of our planet, which have resulted in 20 to 96 percent of some species, families, and genera being eliminated at any one time. Ninety-seven percent of all life that has ever existed on this planet is extinct. The earth has been around for an estimated four billion years and by all estimates will be around for another 500 million years. It seems to me that according to these numbers the earth is 88 percent of its way toward complete extinction anyway and that anything humanity could visit upon it has already happened before at least five times. The earth has recovered each time, only to be just as rich in biodiversity, if not more so, than the previous epoch. What is happening right now to the planet at the hands of humanity and our use, some might say abuse, of technology is not and cannot be the end of the world, as I used to believe. That is far and away beyond our capability. However, we probably are bringing about an end to the world as we know it. Regardless, we are not bigger than life. The earth will recover as it has before after this latest experiment in exploration of consciousness, humanity, created by and for God, has run its course. What is happening that is of much more significance to universal knowledge is that we are experiencing firsthand what the effects of humanity living unbalanced and unconsciously can be,

Notes

and the effects will be—they are—painful. It has been estimated that right now, extinction of species is happening at a pace that rivals any of the mass extinctions ever discovered. Do we think that this is not painful and that the life forms and the systems they depend upon for survival are not suffering for the pollution we continue to pour into our environment? We are learning that fear, in any form, does not work, including the fear that we could be ruining anything, because it only creates what we perceive to be pain as energy balances.

Fearing the end of the world is just more of the same that created the mess we have on our hands. We have an opportunity, and we will exercise this opportunity, to learn from our lessons—not mistakes, but lessons—and be in control of our change or we will have change put upon us by the benevolent collapse of the systems we currently depend upon to support what we are doing. Pain will teach us that we cannot treat each other, ourselves, and our planet the way we have been and expect to be sustained. Pain will protect us from totally destroying everything, even though we could not regardless. Just as children learn to not put their hands too close to a flame, we will learn that we cannot keep living outside the natural system without it leaving us behind. Should we come to recognize that we are a part of instead of apart from our natural world, that we are all in this together, and that our fear is what has brought us to the brink in the first place, we will make the changes because we will accept that we can, because we always have. If not, the world as we know it will collapse while the earth cleanses itself, not unlike what a human body goes through as it detoxifies itself during a sickness, and what is left of humanity will adapt to a new world.

This will, however, not be a waste. Nothing ever is. The knowledge of what happened at the hands of fear will pervade every society that develops out of the change, and everything will be fine. Pain will have done its work. God will have experienced through our experience, and knowledge of aspects of God's creation will be that much more complete. This is such an interesting part. We

51

Notes

are creating all of our pain only to show ourselves that we are in control of creation, even if what we are creating is destructive. We are only showing ourselves through the only means from which any of us truly learn—experience, the amazing power we possess—and during this process the energy we are sending into the universe is being acknowledged and forever changed. Everything is connected, and our choices as reflections of our being grow the universal consciousness. We are all in process, individually contributing to the One, our collective lessons affecting and being effected by all that is. Exciting, yes? I believe it is exciting, all of it, and though I still catch myself criticizing or complaining on occasion I have never been as supportive and accepting a person and only become more so as I leave my old 'self' behind and embrace all that we are and will be.

Notes

"You must be the change you wish to see in the world."
Mahatma Gandhi

These few words, spoken by no less a messenger of God than any to have come before, speak to the wisdom, knowledge, and understanding of who we humans are, and as such the destiny that awaits us. "Being the change" is the key to understanding the integral role we as humans play in the evolution of an emotion-based cycle of consciousness.

By choosing to be the change we wish to see in the world, we are accepting with gratitude the responsibility and effects that we as individuals have on all of our brothers and sisters. We are declaring to the mystery that is life, the song that is the soul, our recognition and acceptance of this responsibility as expression of who we have become for the experience we have had. Through this declaration we pay respect to the sacredness of every human path that has been walked, including our own, every path that is being walked, and every path yet to be defined on Mother Earth. Every path is a unique exploration of creation, a personal remembering of all that is. Only through awareness intersecting with experience, that personal intimate dance with the magic of the mystery that is life, can knowledge add to the emotion that is the mosaic of consciousness, encouraging and facilitating change and growth personally for humanity and our universe.

Being the change pays homage to this understanding, because its very foundation is the understanding that we have the power to mold our reality with our thoughts, and that not only can we exercise this power but we always have, and we are limited only by our ability to see who we are. As we are the change, we recognize the quantum construct of the universe and the connectedness of the All, and pledge to contribute the only way we can, the only way we need to, to the greatest good for all. Because of the intimate infinite connection of ourselves to each other and the All, this information, this energy, is distributed throughout the Infinite, via the beating of our hearts, to affect all that can be. This is not

Notes

philosophy; this is physics, which in turn can be adopted as a philosophy, a perspective to see the world by, for those who are ready to adopt it. Interestingly, by being the change, those who have come before to show us the way have energetically paved "the way," so to speak, for the raising of consciousness in those who are awaiting their turn. The constant of creation, change, is thus inevitable as experience begets wisdom. Wisdom in turn is used by those who have made the journey to that point to provide the light by which those who follow may be guided. We are all here for each other, because ultimately we are all each other.

For any tool to be used consciously, it must first be recognized consciously that the tool is possessed. Being the change is truly possible only because humans can and will come to recognize that we are the power that effects change in our lives, therefore taking responsibility for who we are and what is happening in our lives. This is of course no mean feat, and just this recognition alone is a shifting point in any person's life. To no longer feel like a victim, to know and exercise the power of our thoughts, accepting all the responsibility that comes with this awesome authority, changes lives, personally and collectively. Leaving behind the limited, stifling perspective of victim as one moves into the expansive, liberating role of co-creator is a change noticed by everybody and anybody, and never a word needs to be shared. Shed is the perspective that life is happening to us, happening in a way beyond our control, left to the fickle fate of chance and percentages. Instead, in its place is the knowledge that we are happening to life, that the mystery through which the balance of energies and the emotions that produce effect is truly within our control and always has been; we have only been experiencing its discovery. Every circumstance, remembered and forgotten, was a cause and/or effect, all connected, all created, and all existing to show us the power we possess to create them in the first place. Manifesting all, in every moment, we look back over our lives to recognize every step as having been integral to our arrival and awakening, and are thus restored and humbled to have ever been afforded the opportunity to begin with.

Notes

Being the change is all about gratitude, having come to understand that who we are has never been apart from but rather always a part of. The consciousness of God has been arranged in a pattern that not only facilitates the creation of life but in turn is sustained by that same creation, through the evolution of knowledge fed by experience. Gratitude is appreciation realized, manifested, and set into motion, giving back to life for the life that has been given. It is humility in realizing the amazing opportunity to live and give that has been afforded us. It is knowing that all can be done and all is being done as we are released by the recognition provided by awakening into who we are. Thus being the change ushers in a new world of acceptance and allowance, the home of conscious creation. The change in the world for which we are all waiting, a world of love and freedom and support for all to exercise their dreams and manifest their potential, begins individually, as just one more step on the mountain of human experience.

As we come to embrace the truth of who we are, we do so aided by our understanding of sponsoring thought. Sponsoring thoughts are the beliefs that define our reality. In essence they are our instructions to creation of who we are being, which in turn the universe uses to support us unconditionally because we are that loved. Fear-based sponsoring thought brings us fear reflecting experience, and love-based beliefs create a loving experience. The more consistent our beliefs and desires, the more consistent our reality. The more in line our beliefs are with our desires, the more effective our lives are, the less complicated and therefore straightforward. Sponsoring thought does not tell all of the story that is a human life, but it provides a basis for a deeper understanding. When we have come to know, completely and unequivocally, that everything is fine, that it always has been because all experience contributes to growth and knowledge, this is the energy that we give back to the mystery that is the universe. We do so knowing that everything that has caused pain and suffering in ourselves and all of humanity has resulted from a sponsoring thought that everything is not fine, that there is something to fear. This same thinking translated into doing creates

Notes

a negative ripple effect into the universe through the process of karma, just as loving thoughts create a positive supporting ripple effect. Being the change, being at peace, reflecting harmony: when we share the truth of love and freedom as expressions of who we believe we are, we give this not just to ourselves but to all of our brothers and sisters. Whether we recognize it or not, we are one with One, so there is no alternative other than all of us affecting each other all the time.

The universe responds to the power of our thoughts in kind, as it always has. But when we are creating consciously, we can do so because we accept the responsibility for the effects of our thoughts as the necessary balance for the authority to have them in the first place. Fearful thinking and unconscious beliefs still serve a purpose, by showing us that they do not work in supporting our dreams and desires as well as revealing to us the process that we can use and in fact the process that we are, love seeking love. We possess the mechanism through our thoughts, words, and actions that creates our shared reality. We truly were created in the image of God and display our likeness not so much by what we create but simply by virtue of the fact that we do. What we create only testifies to how far along we are on our journey of remembering, and "being the change" is a measure that we are arriving home, a place in which we become not only much less dangerous to each other but much less so to ourselves.

Being the change, recognizing the connectedness of it all, blesses the mind-body connection and the service the body provides as we move from unconscious to conscious creation. Our bodies, as gifts from God, register the ease with which we accept ourselves and all of creation. Barometers of our sponsoring thought, human bodies cannot help but reflect who we think we are. As we are the change, our bodies reflect our acceptance and allowance because they in turn are allowed. They are allowed to do what they do best, which is to protect and repair themselves. Even more important than the food we eat or the liquid we drink or the air we breathe or the exercise we provide are the thoughts we put

Notes

into our bodies. Our bodies, as a reflection of creation, respond just as unerringly and without prejudice to our sponsoring thought as creation, mirroring who we think we are because they love us that much. As we come to understand who we are, as we come to love ourselves, our bodies in every aspect reflect this love, radiating health, well-being, and happiness just as they do the opposite under opposite conditions. Disease in our lifetime is the result of dis-ease in our thoughts. We know we are coming to understand this relationship when our response to illness is one of responsibility. We also know we are moving closer to this understanding when we begin to actively give thanks to our body for all that it does in every facet of our lives and treat ourselves with gratitude at every opportunity.

We do not have to be the change we wish to see in the world, but we do eventually understand that inevitably we will when we possess the wisdom of experience to support such a perspective. As a course of our growth this is our destiny, and it seems like it is a choice only because we have ever held the perspective that any of what we do is. Being the change is not a destination or goal for humanity; rather it is simply a sign along the path of our journey of how far we have come and how close to home we are. In a world where all exists only as an expression in relation to everything else, this place is experienced as so much more peaceful, and powerful because of what we have denied ourselves in the past. Thus, in being the change we recognize, accept, and embrace every step that came before, even though it reflected an attitude of anything but being the change. Resistance, rejection, and judgment are the preserve of the unconscious, the experience of which is absolutely critical in support of acceptance, allowance, and freedom. This is the power of love. That which is not is fear. The experience of the latter invariably leads to the former because of knowledge gained from that experience. We are perceivers, we are students, humanity is upon a path of remembering who we are, and every step is critical in support of the next and as a reflection of the prior. We don't always know

Notes

this, but we will come to know this, from not knowing. Being the change recognizes the sacredness of all experience and as such provides us personally with a valuation and validation from which we can view and treat and love all of creation. When we can truly be the change, then everything will have changed.

Notes

HOPE

Hope: Expectancy; Longing; the feeling that what is wanted can be had or that events will turn out for the best. dictionary.com

I have no desire to offer anybody any hope whatsoever. Hope can exist only in a worldview where circumstances can turn out differently from what is prejudged to be appropriate or desirable. It is not my wish to indulge this reflection, this shadow of fear that anything can ever be or ever has been in the human experience less than perfect, from the ultimate perspective of God and ourselves as an expression of God.

How many books and treatises have I read by the likes of the Dalai Lama, Eckhart Tolle, Don Miguel Ruiz—the list could go on—who offer their sincere advice about how we can have hope in the face of the fear and suffering being visited upon the human race by the human race. Providing advice on how to live a meaningful life can come only from a perspective that lives can be lived that are not meaningful. Understanding God the way that I do, this simply can't work for me. I cannot imagine God having the inclination to ever waste an opportunity. If everything is for a reason, then there has to be a reason for everything. I am in no way criticizing any of these authors—or any others, for that matter—for their efforts to remedy the human condition. They too are exactly in the place they are supposed to be, contributing to human knowledge and God's knowledge with respect to what works and does not work as reflected by the experience we are having as compared with the experience we say we wish to be having. Hoping, trying to provide hope, wishing against hope for things to turn out differently, in my view is a proclamation to the universe that life is anything but perfect. The success of new age spirituality and old age religion lies in their ability to offer answers to people who feel there is something wrong with the world, their world. The sponsoring thought supporting the notion of hope

Notes

is that life could be anything but perfect, and hope offers the notion that such won't be the case, though it could. But then this leaves me asking the question, "How can we expect the universe to provide us a world of perfection when we are entertaining the possibility that it is not?" In a reality where human thought is supremely creative, living and creating from a perspective of hope is only dooming us to experience less than what we desire because we are even entertaining the idea that we can experience less in the first place.

I know that there are readers right now—the quicker ones, the ones who are seeing farther only because they have traveled farther up the mountain that is human experience—who are questioning me, ready to accuse me of an inconsistency here: "If everything has a purpose because there is a purpose for everything, how can you the author say this on one hand and on the other criticize others for anything, even entertaining and espousing the idea that there is hope for humanity, because this too, according to your own definition of creation, must be serving a purpose." If you are one of those who are asking this question on behalf of everybody, let me thank you. You are absolutely correct. Hope does serve a purpose, and it is the same purpose that is fulfilled by fear: it shows us what works by exposing that which doesn't. And again, it is not my intention to criticize only support. If we don't want pain and suffering in our lives, how can we possibly achieve this when we are entertaining that it does and even can touch who we are. The deepest truth, of course, is that with the power of our thoughts we create lives that are self-fulfilling prophecies. I wish to celebrate all aspects of life because I recognize that all is integral. It has to be if you can see a God that is in complete control of Her creation. I do not question the motives of any human who truly desires to help another human being. We are here to support each other because we are in a sense only helping ourselves. I am, though, questioning the efficacy of many who in their attempts to help others may not be doing so, at least not directly. Fearing fear, for example, never defeats fear; it only feeds it. Fear is not to be feared; it only needs to be understood. From understanding, fear can be transformed,

Notes

because that which is accepted disappears, whereas that which is rejected persists. In acceptance we are saying to the universe that everything is fine, in which case this is what is offered back to us. In rejection we are believing that circumstances are less than desirable so we experience life as such and get more of it from our benevolent supporting source. I didn't make the rules; I just apply them. Fire was never extinguished by adding fire. Fear will never be overcome by trying to avoid it or eliminated because we are afraid of it. Fear can only be loved to death. Love is but another word for understanding. We are all living meaningful lives with God's complete attention on all of us in every moment. The only difference is that part of the time we don't know our lives have meaning, and this inevitably leads us to knowing that they always have been completely meaningful.

Look at our world today. There is so much worry, so much concern, so very much caring about what will become of this planet because of the direction we have chosen through the use of our technology. Pollution, environmental degradation, military buildup and conflict—all contribute to the level of worrying and concern humans are feeling and exploring. New generations are wondering just how wise previous generations were to have created such a mess. They question why they should listen to those who clearly do not have the answers, as evidenced by the situation they will leave behind for the next to clean up. I believe we are figuring out that worrying is not the same as caring. God cares deeply, but I don't for a second believe that God worries. God can see how all of what we are exploring is filling in the bottom of the mountain of human experience. God can see that all that is, is for a reason. Balance is the basic tenet of all physical law, and for the top of the mountain to exist, to be able to see as far as it permits, to see what God sees, the bottom must be there—relatively speaking the opposite of the top—to provide balance, support, appreciation, and knowledge. As we collectively move closer to the top of the mountain, all the advice we are given about how to reach those lofty heights will be seen as just one more example of having had to exhaust those paths that only have a dead end so that

Notes

we could find our own. Once we have found our own, from that height and that perspective, fear and its assistant, hope, will be appreciated for what they too provide, indirectly. We will see that the outcome has never been in doubt, though it needed to seem that way, and from our acceptance and love of everything in the past, represented by the bottom of the mountain, our sponsoring thought will usher in the new age where acceptance and allowance are the attendants of truth.

The new age is happening as we speak, so to speak. Humanity is moving to the place collectively as we individually are waking up to who we are. Trying and doing is being replaced by the understanding that only being truly brings about our desired results. Being always has. The universe responds to sponsoring thought, which is another term for being. As we move to that place—and we can do so only one step at a time because each step needs the experience and knowledge of the previous one to support it—we instinctively and naturally move closer to God. From our seeing farther comes acceptance and allowance. We let go of the idea that we need to control anything outside of ourselves for fear that it cannot turn out properly without us guiding it. In its place starts to grow the understanding that everything can reflect only what we believe and that for everything to be okay, we just have to know that everything is okay, including and especially when it seems to be otherwise. There is no way to fool the universe, and no way of "putting one over" on God so to speak, though it is instructive to try. Indulgences have been sold in the past, and offers are available today on the Internet promising to "Change your life in ten minutes with this SECRET long-lost technique." As we move through the process that is the circle of life, understanding the process becomes available to us, as does its purpose. This is our destiny, but the destiny matters only while we are "trying" to get there. Once we are there, in that place of understanding, where we are no longer matters because the illusion of "having a destination" has been shattered by the view afforded from where we find ourselves. Did you get that? Where we find OUR SELVES. We then know that every

73

Notes

step along the way is just as important as the step before and the step after. Prejudice evaporates, as does rejection and resistance in the light of love and understanding as we move into the realm of God and the higher truths available because of our being.

Everything—all information, energy, and knowledge—is waiting for us, and hope ultimately has very little bearing on the matter. This is our destiny. Then again our destiny is also to choose to go back into the mix of having forgotten who we are when we are ready again to experience the thrill of remembering who we are. Some are ready for truths that others are not. We are not all in the same place of our evolution at the same time, and again, the only value in being anywhere is that which we decide is serving who we believe we are and what meaning we attach to it. In God's eyes all is necessary and all is celebrated; after all, just having the opportunity to have any experience is preferable to having none. Obviously God feels this way; otherwise She would not have created all of this, including hope, which by the way will be shed like a jacket in the afternoon sun, not because anybody has enabled us to, but because we are ready to give this to ourselves, in our own due course.

Notes

You Can Lead a Horse to Water ...

I have wondered at length why Jesus, who came to save the world of humanity from itself some two thousand years ago, has not been back in the same capacity since. It seems only natural that somebody who could rise from the dead, as he did, could also control where and when he comes back as a human, as I am sure he did when he came as Jesus. So why then has he not come back? Certainly we have not learned what he came to teach us—at least it seems that way to me. We don't, for example, Do unto others as you would have them do unto you, from Luke 6:31, not by any measure. The Golden Rule, as this saying is known, is also found in Matthew 7:12, and reads as follows: So in everything, do to others as you would have them do to you, for this sums up the Law and the Prophets. Jesus came and chose also to give his life in the attempt to bring teaching to the children of God, though it seems that even this extreme act on his part was unsuccessful. Did he just quit? Did Jesus give up on humanity, leaving us to our own devices as a lost cause with no chance for redemption? It could almost seem so, but this answer does not work for me.

I believe that Jesus has in fact always been with us and will always be with us. Until the last soul has remembered itself, Jesus the shepherd will choose to provide His light and love for the children of God, his brothers and sisters. However, I believe that after His experience in Galilee, Jesus chose to work for humanity in a different capacity because he learned from that experience. Some may read these words and take offense, seeing Jesus as perfect and therefore not needing to learn anything; they may believe that to even intimate that such could or would be the case is blasphemous. If that is the way anybody chooses to react to this writing, all I can say in my defense is so be it. Believe what you wish, as a true reflection of how you see the world, your place in God's creation, and who you are in relation to Jesus. But please know, I will do the same. I believe that Jesus was not above learning, the same as we all do all the time, as God does in every moment, having knowledge made complete from experience, vicariously through

77

Notes

Her creation, especially humanity. What Jesus learned, I believe, is that despite his best intentions, in spite of his knowledge and power with respect to who we are, he was not bigger than the process, the process of life. Even in his attempt to save us from ourselves, it makes sense to me that he was learning that not only was there nothing to be saving us from in the first place but nothing could be more important than the process, because it is the process, the circle of life, that is paramount. It is the alpha and the omega, the light and the dark, the means and the end. Even Jesus did not fully appreciate that only from experience do we really learn, that only from learning do we grow. There can be no shortcuts and no links eliminated from the chain, because without the circle of life there is no life. Without learning the "hard way," there is no learning, because there is no experience to support it. Life cannot be shown as it has to be seen.

To believe that we need to be saved, or that conscious living is better than unconscious living, is only to repeat Jesus' mistake. It underscores just how important it is for all of us to learn for ourselves. Ultimately, because we exist within a closed, inclusive system, created by God to explore consciousness on behalf of God, the only reason we can believe that we could ever be lost or need saving is that God created the possibility for this subjective perception, not because it really exists. Without knowing dark we cannot know light. Jesus learned this through his experience. Jesus also learned that you can lead humans to the truth, but you can't make them know it. I believe that many of the writers and light bearers for the raising of consciousness on this planet are in the process of learning this same lesson. They have found for themselves a path that has led them to who they are. They know that they are children of God, co-creating their reality with the power of their thoughts, from the foundation of their beliefs. They have discovered what is meant in Matthew 17:20, which says, "I tell you the truth, if you have faith as small as a mustard seed, you can say to this mountain, 'Move from here to there' and it will move." What they are missing, however, is what Jesus learned the last time he was here on earth in a conspicuous role. Yet even

Notes

in their not completely understanding that they cannot protect people from themselves, they are learning that such is the case, for themselves from their perspective and for God. It is kind of like those people who have discovered a wonderful diet that works perfectly for their own metabolism and physiology and then write a book to encourage everybody to follow the diet because it really works. "Just look at me," they say, and yet how many people who buy the book and follow the diet to the letter fail to experience the same results? Lots! Those people trying to follow a diet that is not suited for their bodies have not been led down a garden path; those of us who have tried to apply the principles of the "enlightened" writers of our generation without success have not either. In the failure to achieve the same results by following the recipe somebody else has figured out, we are one step closer to coming upon our own, because we come to realize that for ourselves only our own path will do. Learning that if humanity does not do something about the way we live and treat each other and treat ourselves, we will end humanity as we know it, is only moving one step closer to understanding that there never was anything to be afraid of in the first place. Fear begets fear, and we need not be anywhere except exactly where we are, because even without knowing it, wherever we are, having whatever experience we are having, is supporting us moving through consciousness. Try putting a value on educational grade levels, attempting to convince someone that a higher grade is better than a lower one. Without the learning provided at the lower grades to support higher understanding, there could not be the latter. Without the opportunity provided by the higher grades to come into larger truths there would be no need for the lower grades. The grades of education exist because of each other, for each other, and it is the same of all experience, including thinking the opposite is the case—that grades in education or experience can exist exclusively or have value that is different from others.

Even a seeming step backward is always a step forward, because learning what doesn't work is as fundamental as learning what does. The point is that in a world where everything happens

Notes

for a reason—because there is a reason for everything—it is just as important for complete knowledge to know how things don't work as it is to know how they do. Being given directions that do not apply to us, and us taking them, hoping for relief from our current situation is every bit as valid and important an experience as coming to realize that all the answers have been within us from the beginning anyway. Believing that it is the type of experience we are having that is most important and then driving ourselves to seemingly early deaths from the stress of trying to have and then hold on to said experience is as instructional as coming to realize that all experience ultimately is for learning and growing and thus fueling the climb up the mountain that is human experience. Jesus learned this. Perspective provides appreciation. Knowing what a muddy path is allows us to fully love a dry one. Thinking that there is anything to be saved from, that there is peril at all in what we do, say, or think, provides an opportunity to embrace how truly safe we in fact are, in all ways, in God's creation.

As part of our path we come to these truths, but just as the top of a mountain needs the bottom to support it, not knowing, being afraid that we could somehow "miss the boat," trying to control a system that does not require any control, all contribute to understanding, growth, and consciousness as we know it and are coming to know it. Jesus learned this, that even fear does not have to be feared, and he will be here again to lead us when the time is right, when the time has come for humans to embrace and understand his teachings, because we will have the experience of knowing what doesn't work to support the experience of what does. Heaven on earth is our destiny, and we are steadily, methodically, and purposefully working to this place on the circle of life, the never-ending chain of consciousness that is God.

Notes

Twin Flames

There is a perspective of our souls, a relationship of personalities, that is explained by the concept of the twin flame. It is thought that when souls first leave Source, they do so complete in the knowledge of who they are, from where they came, and how they will journey back. Our souls "know" and remain complete in that knowledge of what they are and the role they are playing within creation, and therefore are in perfect relationship with Source. Our souls know they are an aspect of God. I believe that when our souls leave Source, there is in effect a mini big bang that takes place, a dismembering of wondrous, perfect proportions, the result of which is the spreading of conceptual knowledge, energy, and information throughout all of the universe that in turn will mix and join with all the energy and information that has been issued forth by all other souls. This organization of energy, the power behind the synchronicity that becomes our lives, is both the magic and mystery of life that we know exists, that we are always looking for, that is always right in front of our noses if we know what we are looking for. From the seeming chaos created by the "random" expulsion of information and then its coalescence into the lives we live, the world we create is the universe finding its balance, is the wonder of it all.

So our soul—the intermediary, our very life force that can never be destroyed, that from which our connection to Allah is constant and forever, from which we came and to which we will always return—has a role to play in the process of life. On behalf of creation our souls guide our personalities, all of our lives, throughout the labyrinth of this dimension in a physical dance choreographed and in concert with all other souls. Every experience we have is not so much a discovery for our souls—though it seems that way to us personally because we can compare the feeling of emptiness with the feeling of coming to know—as it is a remembering, and contributes to the mosaic that is our soul. Our soul is responsible for the completion of itself, and we are the tools with which it completes this task.

85

Notes

The use of the twin flame is absolutely critical to the fulfillment of this purpose, some believe. Twin flames, however, are not to be confused with soul mates or members of a soul family.

Soul mates and soul family members are personalities representing the separate souls with whom we have contracted to remember who we are. As such, souls move through various lives working with other specific souls to create energy imbalance and then must achieve balance with only those same souls. Karmic debt and credit can be issued by and paid back only through the interaction of the souls with whom all originated. As such we go through our lives interacting with representatives and personalities of the same souls with whom we created everything in the first place. Again, how this is done is the mystery and magic of life. All of us have met people in our lives toward whom we immediately have very strong feelings for some unexplainable reason. These feelings are a knowing based upon a remembering from concurrent lives*[1]. They are signals we give to ourselves that something—a balancing—is about to take place. Though we seldom if ever can know what or how events will transpire to achieve the work that we were meant to do in that particular space and time, the remembering or feeling of having known somebody before is usually a clue to this process coming into our lives. Soul mates, the romantic notion of finding with another person permanent lasting love that can provide for a lifetime what only true agreement can represent, exist, of course. Our personal search for this circumstance is but another indication of how far up our mountain of experience we have remembered. Believing that this particular scenario is "better" at the exclusion

---

1   *Just as an aside, I use the term *concurrent lives* rather than the term *past or future lives*. I know that from our linear perspective of past, present, and future, it seems like our souls' lives are being lived one after the other, but ultimately, from our souls' perspective this is not the reality. Instead, our souls could be thought of in the terms of a book, a book in which each page represents a life lived. Each page may be read separately, but they do not come into existence when they are read; they are already there, lying one on top of the other, waiting to be experienced and used, actually all happening at the same time in the eternal moment of now.

Notes

of all others merely points to the reality that we are not seeing the integrity of all experience, but that will come. Seeing the necessity for another to complete us, thus looking outside ourselves for this, is being just that: without. When we can be within, we will know that we have moved to that place of completion that allows. However, just as no link in a chain matters more than any other, we needn't attach value to one perspective over another, unless we do. Ultimately everything matters, including attachment of value, if only to show us what doesn't work.

What all relationship does for us is serve as a reflection for ourselves of who we are "being." Where in the spectrum of human emotion, lying somewhere between the extremes of love and fear, are we finding ourselves with respect to the person we are in relation to? If we worry about or for the person in question, we are closer to the fear end of things, and depending upon the amount of worrying we do and the various forms that worrying can take from mild concern to complete paranoia, we show ourselves the degree to which we are fear, in relation to them. Caring about somebody and not worrying but instead showing constructive, confident support in his or her self-expression is of course "being" on the loving end of the spectrum. The degree with which you are being love will be exemplified by the freedom you allow yourself to give that other person. The more freedom, the more love, because freedom is but another word for love. The more freedom you are giving another, the more you are loving yourself, and this will be reflected back to you, to us, through the relationship.

This in a nutshell is how our souls work with each other. The twin flame, however, is how our souls work with themselves. When our souls first leave Source, they split into two, creating two polar opposites, the yin and the yang, if you will, that vibrate exactly the same and know each other only as being complete—like the electron and the proton that create a neutral, balanced atom. The twin flames create a complete soul when they come back together. This is why romantic relationship is so important for humanity and our innate perspective of it is one of balance, harmony, and

Notes

permanency. We are literally practicing through our personal relationships for that time when we can become one again with our "other half," our twin flame. However, when twin flames encounter each other during a personal passage, they rarely have an easy time of it. In fact these relationships can be the most difficult ever experienced. The attraction they share for each other is like no other attraction they will experience, yet the revulsion they have for each other can be just as intense. It is important to understand that twin flames know each other only in their perfect, complete, and balanced state. Experiencing the other, who from a vibration perspective is a mirror image, as anything less than perfect simply cannot be tolerated, because in that mirror image they cannot escape or compensate for being less than perfect themselves. They truly hate loving each other because they have no control over the attraction, but being together brings no satisfaction, only irritation because of the perfect mirror they are for each other. In fact because of their perfect vibration, they magnify in each other beyond reasonable proportion any fear that either of them continue to carry in their lives, and it is this fear magnified that ultimately, most often, tears their relationship apart. They are left wondering, totally confused and in shock, what the heck just happened, not even recognizing who they were during the relationship. This emotional tug-of-war serves as the impetus for change and awareness and knowledge like no relationship that either of them will ever experience could. Having been through it, I accept its purpose though I would not wish the effects of this relationship upon anybody. Despite the freedom that can be available on the other side, should you survive the experience, which fortunately I did—this book is but one more testament—it is not at all fun, only work and inevitable. This experience truly reflects that nobody can protect us from ourselves, even and especially ourselves.

Twin flames are seldom meant to be together for very long. Few are emotionally and energetically strong and complete enough to use this relationship for any other purpose than to propel them into the next phase of their life, into the next stage of their

Notes

soulful remembering. To stay together is but an indication of how complete these two already are, but whether twin flames stay together or not or ever even meet for that matter does not in any way define the success of this relationship. Twin flames are always aware of each other on an energy level. Whether they come together in a lifetime or are even alive at the same time, twin flames are always aware of their other half, moving, growing, and discovering together as each grows individually in response to individual experience. Once they have met on a personal physical level, the connection is complete for that lifetime, regardless. As one climbs the mountain that is human emotion, the other sees what the first is seeing. Their relationship is as elemental and transcending as any that exist, because it reflects the relativity and duality that is life. Twin flames are the light and the dark, the head and the tail that make the coin, the hot and the cold that conjure temperature. Being the yin and the yang, reflections of each other that allow for the experience upon which life is based, this is the fundamental relationship that forms the foundation of existence, upon which all others can and do rest. This is why we will always be looking, always are looking, for that person to complete us. Of course we can and do discover who we are on our own with our soul mates and our soul families, but all of this is done to prepare us for that which makes life possible, our coming together to complete once we are complete. For myself, the coming together of twin flames is not unlike the coming together of awareness and experience. Each is necessary to create complete knowledge. The whole is greater than the sum of its parts and represents this same process, the process that is God.

Notes

Letting Go

Humanity is truly a three-part being: spirit, mind, and body. As such, each separate aspect of who we are reflects, affects, and is represented within each of the other two parts. Far from being separate, the three parts that make up a human being are so intimately connected that they really cannot be discussed accurately except in relation to and as part of one another. One hundred trillion cells, on average, combine and live and die, only to be replaced and provide the opportunity for a soul to physically experience, perceive, create, and otherwise interact with other souls and all of God's creation. Yet once the soul has reached the point where its work is complete in a particular body and leaves, our cells without the life essence of our soul perishes, and thus begins the process of giving back all the energy borrowed from Mother Earth for us to come into being to begin with. A new body is conceived and begins to grow and becomes home for the soul for which it was intended. That soul brings with it the memories of all concurrent lifetimes, memories that come to reside in the cells of the body. These memories, represented as emotion, have become physically represented within the karmic dance of synchronicity to play out their effects and to "be cause" in a lifetime whose sole purpose is to provide the opportunity for the personality hosting this awareness to awaken— not for the sake of awakening per se but for the change through knowledge gained from experience that awakening provides the circle of life to be able to continue to change.

In a book titled **Messages from the Body**, author Narayan Singh Khlasa writes the following:
Every (physical) condition in our lives exists because there is a need for it in one way or another, either on the time-space level or on the soul level. The symptoms, reactions or conditions are the outward effect of the inner (emotional) condition of the individual. A specific sickness is the natural physical outcome of specific thought patterns and/or emotional disharmonies. They are the coded messages from the body to the effect of what is happening and what needs to happen. In effect, then, illness and ailments teach us, expand us, and move us on. pg 10. 1991

Notes

Messages from the Body, chronicles the psychological underpinning of all human ailments, including the relationship between specific body parts and their emotional ties, and types of death and accidents as they manifest themselves in physical injury. I know of therapists who successfully use this "bible" in their work, and I have benefited from the insights provided by this text. It is very easy for me to recognize and accept that thoughts are energy and affect us physically, through the response of our brain to the emotion of our thoughts, whose electro-chemical reaction then triggers cause and effect in the body. Personal experience tells me this is the case, and I have witnessed healings after exhausting western medical approaches to providing relief and cures. Once the psychological and emotional trauma was revealed and the required energy healing was provided, my physical body was allowed to do what it naturally does very well: heal itself.

Having said this, let me preempt the naysayers by discussing the placebo effect. It has come to my attention that pharmaceutical companies are trying to devise methods to understand and then minimize if not eliminate the placebo effect. Just as I have heard it said, "Oh, it's all in your mind," the placebo effect testifies to the power of belief. It has been proven, much to the chagrin of the pharmaceutical manufacturers, that people can "believe" themselves into being cured. Subjects have been given sugar pills and told that they are receiving the latest breakthrough in medicine designed to cure their illness and their bodies have responded accordingly. Sometimes the number of participants responding to the sugar pill therapy has been as high as 30 percent. It can easily be understood why corporations whose business depends upon humanity being sick would be just a little wary of such research and do everything to try to eliminate this competition to their ability to generate profits. I on the other hand see the placebo effect as one more crystal clear example of the mind-body connection. I offer this information because somebody could say in response to my relating my personal experience, "Perhaps your alternative medical approach worked where the western medical approach failed because you believed

Notes

in the former and rejected the latter; thus your success and/or failure was only a self-fulfilling prophecy." To those who would offer such an observation, my only response is "Yes!"

To me it makes no difference what type of therapy we seek, including the therapy that does not work, because again—and I risk sounding like a broken record—even that which does not work has worked by eliminating one more avenue in a process that will eventually expose our truth. Regardless, my point here is not to substantiate one medical approach at the expense of another but to support the idea that our beliefs directly affect our biology and thus our physical experience. This mind-body connection is completely examined by Dr. Bruce Lipton in his groundbreaking book **The Biology of Belief.** Dr. Lipton, a cellular researcher, claims that our beliefs affect not only our biology and health but our very genetics. In his eloquent argument, supported by some thirty years of research, Dr. Lipton explains how our genetics change to support our cells' ability to perceive the world outside themselves when presented with a new stimulus for which they currently lack the ability to respond. Dr. Lipton maintains—and he discusses at length the placebo effect—that instead of trying to minimize it we should be exploring ways to best take advantage of it, because obviously it is real. Our thoughts shape who we are, emotionally, spiritually, and physically, and to control our thoughts is to control our lives.

Dr. Paul Pearsall, in his book **The Heart's Code,** further examines the mind-body connection from the perspective of an organ transplant surgeon who has directly witnessed the effects of inherited memory by his transplant patients—not in all of them, but in enough to provoke the belief that cells carry memory. He provides anecdotal evidence of patients having memories after receiving their transplants that they otherwise cannot account for. Those memories have proven to reflect the lives and experiences of their organ donors, although the recipients do not know their identity. He also provides his own very compelling argument that we humans are all connected through the energy

Notes

of our heartbeats and that we are all immersed in each other's energy throughout our planet and into the universe. Perhaps Gandhi was aware of this connection when he encouraged us to "be the change." Regardless, Dr. Pearsall, coming from a western scientific approach along with Dr. Lipton and many others, I am sure, is lending his voice to what is obvious to me: that our thoughts affect who we are physically and that in turn, who we are affects our thoughts.

Imagine a body that has been constantly immersed in the feelings evoked by war and bloodshed: a fetus conceived and then developing in the chemical reaction to constant fear generated by his mother's reaction to her world, only to be born into this world where any moment could bring an end to his life or the lives of his family and friends. How could this body not reflect the reality of constant fear? Emotionally and psychologically a person in this type of circumstance would have to reflect a "kill or be killed" attitude and have a physiology that reflected and supported this reality. Dr. Pearsall points out that every thought we have has one of two effects on our brains: the thought either supports existing neural pathways because we have had the thought before or new neural pathways are encouraged to develop in response to the thought because it is new. Just as our genetics respond to new stimuli, as Dr. Lipton points out, our brains respond to new stimuli as they are meant to. However, because of the mind-body connection there is resistance from our body's to new ideas. Our body's become used to—I would go so far as to characterize this habituation as addiction—certain chemical responses coming from the brain. Just as a body can become addicted to a drug, heroin, THC, nicotine, alcohol, whatever—the substance really makes no difference—our body's become addicted to the chemicals provided by our brains' predictable emotional response. I wonder if our society has not become addicted to adrenaline. This might explain our love of negative news, violence as reflected in the entertainment we choose and the sports we watch, and our support of revenge as a means to balance perceived injustices. But I digress. Our body's do not

Notes

know right or wrong, what works or doesn't work as a judgment or preconception; they simply respond to stimuli, and if we have been offering a body a negative attitude toward life, this is what it will come to expect. When that chemical response stops, it will be uncomfortable and only want what has been provided in the past to be restored. This physiological response of our body makes changing who we are psychologically a challenge, but within the challenge lies opportunity. If there was not this resistance and it was only a matter of changing our minds, then who we are would change incessantly and we would have no physical anchor as to who we are, defeating the purpose of who we are in the first place: spirit, mind, and body.

That which opposes also supports. Just as fear leads to love, challenge provides strength. Having to overcome the physical aspect of who we are to support who we want to be is absolutely critical in our development as conscious, sentient, co-creators of reality. The knowledge of who we are and the confidence provided by this experience provides the foundation from which we can move into our destiny, that of being, conscious children of God. This is what the process of life is meant to do: bring us awareness of the process and take us to a place of change, which is reflected in growth. Life is change, and our spirit-mind-body connection only becomes stronger and of greater value to us in directing the change consciously for having made itself apparent to us. From compromises to our physical health, to the effects of yoga in supporting meditative practice, to denial of our physical requirements to allow passage into the spirit world beyond and the knowledge it would give us, all aspects of life reflect life, how it works, and the process through which it is expressed. What we put into our body is reflected in what we have put into our mind, and our body's support and reflect and guide us as to what is working and not working in harmony with who we ultimately are through the health we enjoy or endure, as a reflection of our being.

So imagine, then, that we comprise 100 trillion cells, all of which have memory and the ability to conceive and react to what is

Notes

around them. I wonder if there is any circumstance in the universe that has occurred, is happening, or is yet to happen, that our body's do not know about? I have heard that each human cell is the equivalent of six gigabytes of memory storage capability. That is a lot of memory, both individually and especially collectively for a human body. The significance of this is that I imagine if we already know everything, every possibility, then our experiences are really not discoveries so much as the remembering I discussed earlier. If our bodies know everything, then by going within we should have access to the All. This makes sense to me. God, the loving, creative, infinite power that God is, that knows of everything because everything is God, has created humanity in Her image, humanity knowing everything, and all that is preventing us from knowing everything is our belief that we don't and can't. One of my favorite sayings is "What does a person who says she can, have in common with a person who says he can't? They are both right." If belief is everything, if God created everything from God's conceptual knowledge, then we are mirroring God as we come to understand that our beliefs create our experience. If creation comes from conception, conception leads to fulfillment of that creation. Experience and knowledge provide and support conception on a higher level for having grown in response to said experience and knowledge and therefore our beliefs are destined to expand as they can, when they will, and our body's will reflect and support all belief, Our souls will not just be witness but will in fact be directing the entire show, lending support and guidance and providing the coordination with all other souls to keep the integrity of the process intact. Just as conception, fulfillment, and knowledge all work together to provide support and growth for one another as part of the creative process, so our body, mind, and spirit reflect and provide the same for one another.

Notes

In Conclusion

"You don't care what anyone else thinks, do you?"
"Papa, I never did."
"That can only be because you believe."
"Yes."
"And how does God speak to you?"
"In the language of everything that is beautiful."

A Soldier of the Great War, Mark Helprin, 1991

There is no advice I can offer anybody about how to live his or her life. To offer any advice would reflect a sponsoring thought or belief that the way they are living their lives is less than perfect. Providing advice exposes those who would feel it there place to give advice. It betrays their belief that anybody, in this case the recipient of their opinion, could or should be anywhere except where their obvious and current knowledge, awareness and experience has brought them. I can't offer any advice about how people should be living their lives differently because I believe God is perfect and that this perfection reflected by and in Her creation means we are all exactly where we need to be, including feeling like we are not exactly where we need to be.

Feeling like we are not where we need to be, that there is something else waiting for us that we just aren't getting, is our recognition of the "homing device" God has encoded in our DNA that guarantees we will always make our way home. Interestingly, it is this same code that encourages us to listen to anybody else who seems to have information we are searching for that may provide us with some relief for the agitation or pain or suffering we are experiencing as a reaction to the need to find ourselves outside ourselves, despite the fact that everything we need is inside of us. In his book **The Alchemist,** Paulo Coelho does a beautiful job of providing a metaphor for how humanity must go through the process of looking outside ourselves so that we can find what has always been within us. Searching outside ourselves, being afraid that we don't have the answers, is what we are doing when we are

Notes

building our foundation for higher truths. This is the bottom of the mountain upon which finding everything inside of us can rest—and make no mistake, just as fear is restless, love is rest.

So, we are all where we need to be, including rejecting that we are where we should be. Nothing matters because everything does. All experience is necessary because it all contributes to change, and life is change, just as change is life. Therefore, trying to get to some place, such as a certain position in a company, or a certain level of sports competition, or living in a particular neighborhood, or being able to join a type of club, or enlightenment, or just making it to retirement as a means to happiness is destined only to show us that happiness is never a place but instead is a choice as a reflection of being. Just in the act of trying to be happy we are telling the universe through our sponsoring thought that we believe we are not; that is why we are having to try in the first place. If trying to get some place is what we are doing, thinking that happiness is waiting there for us upon our arrival, we are simply in the process of finding out that such is not the case. How many people have you heard of who, upon reaching retirement, promptly die? I hear about these souls all the time. They are dying proof that life is about looking forward to any experience, at the exclusion of none, because to set a goal and have nothing to look forward to upon reaching that goal means that our experience has stopped. Happiness may not have been achieved, but knowledge, understanding of what doesn't work, certainly has.

We are wondrous, creative, all-powerful creatures, and it makes no difference to God whether we are creating unconsciously on that half of the circle upon which we are moving away from Her, or creating consciously on that half of the circle where we are moving toward our home. All creation matters, is sacred, and is an expression of the will of God. Whether we know it or not ultimately makes no difference, because everything makes a difference. Just as God does not require the belief of an atheist to continue existing, God does not require us knowing our experience is sacred for it to be so. In God's creation, where everything that

Notes

exists has existed and can exist only because God has created the possibility in the first place, everything is included and nothing is rejected, especially rejection. When we begin moving closer to God, feeling God in our lives because of the natural progression of the process we are a part of and supporting by our very being, we are doing so only because everybody can and will. Any power that any of us have is only representative of the power we all have. This is why Jesus said, in **John 14:12, the works that I do shall he do also; and greater works than these shall he do.** Jesus was trying to remind us of who we are: singular, expressive, creative aspects of God who through our thoughts and body's perceive, conceive, and create our experience, the same as God. We truly were created in the image of God.

I believe that, as stated in **Matthew 5:5, "blessed are the meek: for they shall inherit the earth."** The meek, who will be anything but weak, will be of humility and gratitude, understanding that to truly control change is to allow change, just as God allows all of creation to fulfill its destiny regardless of how reckless or shortsighted it may seem. From the "mess" the world seems to be in will rise the meek to lead humanity into our potential as loving, all-powerful, co-creative partners with God as we usher in the new age. Being meek, these leaders will understand that rejection only begets more rejection and that fear only creates more fear. They will understand the necessity of our recorded history for teaching us primarily what does not work, and instead of rejecting it as ever having been a mistake, accept it for the lessons it has taught us that just as we created the past, we can forge our future. In this way our history will change as our perspective of it changes. I get a kick out of past and current political pundits, very bright individuals who earn a wonderful living and enjoy considerable fame for their insightful, provocative, and often humorous perspectives on how our political and financial leaders are acting in a hypocritical, self-serving, and potentially damaging manner. They see themselves as exposing the problems of the world, thereby contributing to change in the world. I see them as being only part of the lessons we are learning, that fear and its companions, anger and righteous

Notes

indignation, only maintain the status quo, when the status quo is fear based. Fire will never put out fire, just as complaining and finger pointing will never bring people together. The meek will understand and portray this truth. Mahatma Gandhi understood. Mother Theresa understood.

We all innately know that we have to and are finding our own way. When Mahatma Gandhi said, "Be the change you want to see in the world," he was paying homage to this fundamental truth. We can change only ourselves because we can be responsible only for ourselves, and that is enough because it is everything. Each and every life is sacred, finding its individual way back to God, and when we all, or at least enough of us, are at that point in the life process to understand this, the necessity for rules and regulations and laws will evaporate from this understanding of who we are just as a morning dew does from the rising sun. Fear needs support and protection and rules because it is inherently weak. Love needs no such support because love does support as an expression of its strength. We are figuring this out. Our society keeps making more rules, but are we living any more peaceably? Are lives becoming any easier as we continue to chase a social and financial dream whereby we become more and more specialized in the work we do so we can work more and more hours so we can afford to have more and more people doing our work for us? This is especially so when it comes to the raising of our children. This is not criticism, simply observation, and I accept what we are doing as necessary steps to figuring out what we will be doing, what works. Everybody, keep doing exactly what it is you feel is right. Follow your internal compass, because even what seems in retrospect to have been a step farther away from who you are is only one step closer. This is the promise of God.

We are all souls in process, remembering who we are and being life as we celebrate it. From the sixteen to eighteen thousand children a day who die from starvation and malnutrition, to the world leaders who work to keep this circumstance in place we are all souls providing God as we provide ourselves. When we come to

Notes

believe that everything is beautiful just the way it is simply because we can, the beauty can start to be seen. Those thousands of children dying every single day on earth aren't going anywhere. Those souls are coming back. Energy can neither be created nor destroyed, only transformed, and all human experience transforms energy, turning emotion into knowledge, information that will be available to God and therefore throughout the universe forever. Can you imagine forever? That is what you are, that is what we are: we are forever. This is what Jesus tried to teach us when he allowed himself to be crucified: we cannot be killed, we can control our destiny, we all come back and do differently—not better, just differently—as a reflection of how much more of the picture of life we are able to see because of past experience. Trust me, when people are no longer afraid of dying, all the killing will stop. The fear of dying keeps all the killing—all the types of killing—in place, because in the fear one person has control over another and seems to have control over themselves, if only for a moment. This is why we kill, seeking some sort of control—any kind of control— when we feel we have none. This is never more true than during suicide. Whereas a drowning man will grab even a sword to save himself, a completely devalued person will choose to die as their last attempt to salvage control of a life that they feel has gone completely out of control. And still, we can't kill ourselves. Jesus' own suicide, his martyrdom, was not in vain. We are learning this exactly as we need to exactly when we need to, and when we are able to see just how beautiful our world is, it will be. Until then we will learn the power that we are.

Notes

Discovery?

"Look what is here."
She peered from below.
Her chubby and dirty, perfect hand
Held the rock,
The reason for this day.
"Can you see what is in the rock?"
A vague outline, unmistakable.
Millions of years,
Earth changes,
Presence witnessed, a time revealed.
"Look what you have found!"
"But it was never lost."
"But didn't you see it first?"
"Only because it was already there, Papa."
"My child," he wondered, "who are you?"
And not for the first time.
"It was only waiting." She finished her thought.
"Only waiting?"
"Uh huh."
"Waiting for what?"
"Waiting to show me, to show you."
"To show us what?"
"That we can only see what is ready to be seen."
Pausing, pondering.
Is this rock a metaphor for God,
Revealing God's self to us,
When we are ready,
When God is ready?
"Let's look for some more, Hon."
"Okay, but I am not looking."
"No? What then are you doing?"
"Waiting."   01/10/10

Notes

What Is Real?

A planet that will evaporate
With its solar companions,
Earth, this home
500 million years 'til,
4.5 billion years since,
As the Sun, our star
Turns nebulae,
Expands with diminished gravity,
As fuel supply wanes,
To engulf and destroy,
All to which it gave life.
With radiation, heat,
Particle bombardment,
Everything we know,
Will succumb.
So is this real?
What is all of this for?
If everything, someday
Will all cease to exist.
What is real,
Is not, cannot
Be temporary.
But what will last
Forever?
After we, after earth.
Anything?
Something!
This has to matter.   01/27/10

Notes

To Live

What is, to experience?
Is it all the same?
Why are some so content
And others are never?
Striving, searching
Enjoying, relaxing
Nervous, scared
Loyal, secure
Trepidation or confidence,
To what end does this serve?
Should all for a reason
Then is this only a moment?
If we feel we have missed,
Is it still there?
Experience defines
And will always provide,
Sustenance for soul
From which it may grow,
And remember Itself
As it once used to be
After enjoying completely
That which it is not.
To move through the perimeter,
Of limiting belief,
Past the illusion of despair,
Experience is all
To consciousness and life.
Each just our own,
At one time, one place
Everything awaits
In its natural order,
And yet ...   03/10/10

121

Notes

The Crossroads

Traveling through the night,
A moonless night,
Seemingly desolate stretch,
The darkness concealing all that is.
No artificial light,
Save that piercing the shroud,
My headlights define all that is real,
All that matters for now
Then into the next,
And yet there is more,
There is everything, beyond.
Lost in nothing, attention prodded,
Another traveler in the night.
Enveloped by all that cannot be seen,
Beyond the limits of its beam
Perpendicular to my path,
In this seemingly empty space,
We meet, intersect.
Slowing, pausing, giving way
Curiously, grudgingly?
As quickly as we are upon, we are past,
Yet something lingers.
What were the chances,
In all this time, in all this space?
And my understanding grows,
Beyond the limits of my vision.
Experience, that which makes,
My awareness real,
Bears knowledge as its child.
Having come to this crossroad,
Where in the darkness, from this light,
Awareness gives to experience,
What experience gives to it.   01/09/10

Notes

New Year's Eve '09

Suspended the clouds
Hanging so low,
Attend the presence
Of their recent surrender,
Having blanketed complete
The realm beneath
The world in which
I find myself.
Through the calm of this night
Not a breeze to notice
Fireplace smoke
Straight and true,
Meets resting canopy
Its petition accepted
To join as one.

The lake ripples,
Sensing my approach?
Moving black
Against the white rock,
Brushing the shoreline,
Its extent caressed.
I listen, I feel.
The slight waves
Barely waves
Expend themselves at my feet
My attention one
With their collapsing form.

Issuing forth
From distant shore,
Compressed between lake and sky
The light conducted
So light in the dark,
It comes to meet me
Meet anyone.

Notes

Then, with no pretense,
This veil of darkness,
Supports and I listen,
First one, then the second
My brother, my sister
Keepers of the forest at night.
"Pay attention, our brother
And you may hear
This message for you
For everyone
To carry into the next
From this moment forward.
See with our eyes
Through the shroud of deception.
Use your wisdom to know
That which is real!"
I pause to consider
This manner of appointment.
I offer thanks to my brother,
Thanks to my sister,
The owls of the wood.
From their whisper I hear,
With their eyes I see.
Wisdom allows,
Me to accept,
We may all go in peace.
And invariably the lake,
Washes her shore,
As the cloud sits vigil over the night.   01/1/10

Notes

Why

Why try so hard?
Why work so hard?
The effort, the pain,
And for what?
So we can prove to ourselves,
So we can prove to each other?
Does what we believe need defending,
What we think need support?
Truth needs no protection,
Truth stands alone.
Love and freedom provide,
Acceptance and allowance sustain.
So what is it that demands,
That demands who we are
To be so tired,
To wear ourselves out.
That we must die,
Before our own choosing?
Then above all else
Not recognize the loss,
In having sacrificed who we are,
For the sake of who we are not.   01/13/10

Notes

Judgment

In judgment I've sat
Of myself and others.
I have been judged by others,
And myself.
Claiming right
Declaring wrong,
With the certitude of
Blissful ignorance.
In judgment I know,
I have denied
Sacredness of all paths,
Available to embrace,
Conscious conception.
Acceptance for me
Has begun by seeing,
Why I have denied
Myself and it All.
For having revealed
That which no longer works,
I could only discover
That which does.
As all of us will
Just as all of us are
Following our mystery,
All that we are,
So much more,
Than judgment delivers.

Notes

Everything for a Reason

If everything for a reason,
Then a reason for everything.
What may seem to only
Precipitate pain,
Is waiting to be understood.
Suffering is incentive
To let go of belief,
Opening space
To grow.
Pleasure and that
Which could deliver
From truth at its core,
Beyond now
Past those feelings,
Is source for reflection,
What it is, who we are
In relation to it.
Try to hold on to that enjoyed
While running from that which is not so
Or can we see?
Emerging from the shadow
To create our own,
Embracing all when we will
Carried by current of rejection,
To where the memories of experience
Are ours once again.   03/11/10

Notes

Believing Is Being

The late winter wind keened
For that which was
Betraying the futility
Of resisting that to come
Trying nonetheless.
Pulling collar tight
In his own vain attempt
To ward off desperate chill
The son wondered.
"Father, why do people die for their beliefs?"
"To what do you refer?"
"The girl my age who detonated her bomb.
Scattering who she was,
Destroying those who were.
Why?"
"We believe we are our beliefs."
"Are we not?"
"No. We are so much more."
"How, in what way?"
"Perceptions spring from belief.
Experience is defined by perception.
Yet we are not experience,
We have experience.
We are not beliefs, we have beliefs."
"Who are we then?"
"Ultimately, we are the Observer."
"I do not understand."
"Do you see the water, lying on the frozen ground?"
"Yes, Father, I do."
"That water is like our Truth,
It waits.
The frozen ground like our beliefs,
Resists.
Only when the ground is ready
Can the water be absorbed,
And our Truth will bide.
Keep asking your questions, son,
And you will have your answers,
When the warmth of knowing
Has penetrated the chill of not."   01/10/10

135

Notes

Teenagers

How many of us?
All at some point
During a lifetime
Over many lifetimes
Exercise authority
Forsaking burden.
I see this in the teenager
Midst of maturing
From that of a child
Into adult.
During this most
Difficult stage,
Confusion reigns.
Compelled to act,
Exercising anew,
Authority of adult,
Yet afforded protection,
Given to the child.
From those who provided
The shelter still sought,
From ourselves.

I wonder if humanity
Caught in teenage years,
Wanting the freedom
To make our choices,
But not wanting to see
And have responsibility,
For the contribution
Our choices make,
To the world as it is.
So easily blame,
Shed from oneself
To another,
Or instead we blend,
Into the anonymity

Notes

Offered by the whole.
But in this denial,
Continuing to deny,
We mature.
And while our elusion continues,
So does the evidence of our choices keep pace.
Critical mass achieved
From constant contribution,
And the fear of who we are
Can only lead to our freedom.
And in the light of understanding
Denial becomes acceptance,
Just as the teenager becomes adult.
Responding to ourselves,
Allowing what Is, to be,
Thus moving through the destiny,
Basking in the glow,
Of the love that we are.   06/28/10

Notes

He'll Never Change

In a dimension, a reality,
If you will,
Where subjectively, relatively
Only in comparison to another,
Can we provide,
That perception defines
Who we think we are,
Though ultimately we are
A singular perspective of Source.
Still what we believe
Is the filter through which
We perceive and accept,
What it is that surrounds.
That what we say
About another,
More closely reflects
Who we are,
Our thoughts.
The words represent
What is our truth.
As we feel it,
As only we see it.
To condemn another
To proclaim to the universe,
"Oh, he'll never change"
Is perhaps more accurately,
Ultimately the belief,
Life cannot change.
And from this vantage
It is you who would say this,
Who would choose life to stay
Just as it is,
So your beliefs may remain,
And you can avoid
Any change, yourself?   04/17/10

Notes

A New Day

As I lie in bed
Eyes barely awake,
I know he's here.
Churchill's black dog.

Familiarity provides,
From knowing so well,
Small consolation.
My companion now
Is more the constrictor,
To which the pain in my head, my body,
Attest.
Paralyzed I lie,
Emotional torment I am
Physically expressed.
My benevolent servant
Exercising my wishes,
And I am reminded,
From encounters past.
So this time I laugh,
Smiling within.
For awareness of the source
I give thanks.
I use that same sword
The power that delivered,
The love of the Source,
To expand that, I've restricted,
And in mind's eye I behold,
As my body responds,
The captor takes wing.
Flying to the light,
My light now supports,
Beholding the beauty that it is,
Propelled now transformed.
From every cell of my being
With every cell of my being,
I smile, we smile,
At the sight.
Having moved into the imagining,

Notes

Where all begins,
That as the Source
I am too, the Power.
Purpose fulfilled,
My faithful companion,
And I release him for,
Having shown me the way.
And by the grace of God
I receive that,
Which I have given myself
As I rise, released
To meet the new day.   03/29/10

Notes

Doubtless Fear

Can you love your doubt,
Embrace reflection?
As it points you to
The fear held dear.
Exposed through doubt,
For you to see
As it is made known,
Despite veiled attempt
To disguise from the scrutiny,
Of confused reason.
Protecting from itself,
The betrayal of truth,
To mock oneself,
As trivial measure.
The effort is dense
Yet empty indeed,
For even to doubt
Casts a shadow of doubt.
This insidious aspect,
Oxidizing expression of fear,
Inhaled by this vacuum,
Leaving empty and weak,
Its place secure.
Despite parasitic approach,
Such is the façade.
To reveal itself,
To illuminate all,
As shadow
From light.   04/09/10

Notes

Haiku

In wanting we miss
Give to ourselves we receive
We miss still, and yet ...

Just looking fate sealed
In the act alone, proclaim
That we do not have

Every moment
Every moment apart
One moment closer

Smell that in the air?
That's the fear, the fear of life
Working toward love.

Reached for the summit
Yet the view afforded less
Missed the journey there.

Notes

Water of Life

Am I the water
Within the stream,
This stream called life?
Confined as I am within those banks,
Parameters of consciousness
On either side.
Marking as I go,
Where I will go,
Not how I get there,
And we will.
Is my conscious petition
Caught as I may be?
For now in the whirlpool
Or an eddy, to repose,
Current in the sun
Refracting the Father.
In our moments embrace,
To move below,
In dark sediment,
Being, always being.
Moving through, around
That which would confront,
Accepting that which would divert.
Transformed by heat,
Gift from Mother, from Father.
Transported anew,
To heights once imagined.
Recognition, the memory,
Fresh perspective viewed,
New melded façade I am.
Then destined, a choice?
Back I have fallen,
As rain on my Mother,
Or snow on the glacier,
Ultimately absorbed,

Notes

Separate but within
Moving, morphing,
Outwardly, seemingly different
Always the one, I am.
I can't resist
That which lies ahead
I accept and allow,
I trust and love,
The wisdom of each new destiny,
Moving through or around.
Frozen still I expand,
Accepting loss of heat,
I grow beyond,
To split the rock,
As agreed,
That before diverted,
Only around could I move,
And now I will give it release,
Because I can,
Because I will,
Because it asked.
And now I am left to wonder.
"Am I only the water,
Or the rock, too?"   04/24/10

Notes

Thank You, However ...

I have dreamed this dream,
I remember this dream.
In my déjà-vu, this dream,
I remember.
Invitation to join,
I will decline,
Thank you however ...
You have shared this dream,
Watched this same struggle,
Against the web,
The veil between,
Subtle separation.
Your struggle I share,
You have yet to see
Ropes that bind,
Have always been our own.
You need this moment,
In your dream you're caught,
Not the dream that awaits,
Where all waits.
Reason holds fast
Faint promise of your heart you hear
So faint.
Still you hear.
In denial, you affirm,
Eternal bid for freedom,
Holding ever desperately,
Languishing in the struggle,
Still entertain the choice,
That you ever had a choice.
There are none,
We will see,
And from my dream
I but watch.   07/21/10

Notes

Myself | Face

I sit on the ledge
In the shade of the cliff,
The face casting east
From the afternoon sun.

My gaze rests on nothing
I am searching within.
And I wonder aloud,
Though I've only myself,
"Am I more alive
Than I was at the start?
Or is to still be alive,
Enough?"

I reach with my cup
Catching all that I need,
Water falls past,
As I might have been.
What once was the glacier,
Flowing over the edge,
Drop by drop it cascades
Like a lifetime of memory.
Seemingly one,
But each drop its own,
Adjoined yet distinct,
The water reminds
That looks can deceive.

Proceeding, wet thread
The copper lake that I see,
Two miles away,
So connected I feel.
I trace the stream
Survey well-worn path
Testifying the floods,
Of its oft violent past.

Time a contrivance
Obscured relevance here,
As I regard the meadow

Notes

This blanket of green.
Thankfully protruding,
I am safe once again,
On refuge received,
My gratitude offered
And accepted, I'm sure.

The climbers cut rope
Faded knot on the iron,
Driven into the rock,
Determined it remains.
I understand.
The droppings of goat
Sheep have been here
Perhaps seeking shelter
From a scathing chinook,
Or just taking nourishment
Their rest,
As I do.

As I sit, I eat,
Hands curiously calm,
Where moments before,
They were locked in grip,
My fate being considered
Or some form of retreat,
But none could be offered.
As It raged through my body
With each beat of my heart,
I had only one choice,
If I was to survive.

Oblivious to me
Just as I was to it,
Water leapt down the side,
Unconcerned with its fate.
Poetic irony, I suppose,
That was lost on me then
Only few feet away
From perhaps my last breath.

In that moment, forever
Defined by my fear,
That could cost me my life,
One hundred feet

Notes

Just below,
The scree was aware
Discarded rock as it lay
Though indifferent it was,
To receive my body,
Or not.

No rope, no partner,
Not the time for regret,
Aware I breathed
Again and again,
I may not live
But I would not forget,
That it is fear that kills.

As breath became mine
Constricted muscles could move
Where once I was frozen
I now would press on.
Patient surge from within
Around projection of rock,
Relaxed and composed
I was free from myself.

Backpack released
As I settled on glade,
My escape made complete
From the reckless abandon.
Part of me knew
What I'd given myself
Yet I would meet again
The double-edged sword.

That fear like life,
The life from which fear's made real
Will give or can take.
And only waits, unconcerned
For the choice to be made.   01/23/10

Notes

Right or Happy

Who do you know?
Maybe yourself.
Anybody, everybody
Who would rather be right,
Than happy?
Just to be able
To look at and say,
With a sense of certitude
A hollow satisfaction,
"I told you so."
Of course you are correct,
We all are, can you see?
Creating disasters,
Then bask in consolation
Of supported belief,
Even, especially,
When that same belief
Does not reflect desire.
Small consolation, indeed!,
Is the world to us.
That moment is waiting,
That singular moment will come,
When understanding awakes,
As if by this light.
Reality can't but
Expose our belief,
This is the universe
The power we are.
Then being right
Will fade in the relevance
As belief and desire
Become one.

Notes

All the Same

Seeking happiness,
Or seeking relief,
Amplifying joy,
Or minimizing pain,
Where are we at?
What do we believe?
Assisting ourselves,
Higher places, and purpose,
Defending ourselves,
From the threats we perceive.
Moving within,
To discover creation,
Looking without
And feeling the same.
Where are we at?
Do we know?

Notes

To Stand

In judging part,
All is judged.
In rejection at all,
So do we God,
For all is the One.
Acceptance of this,
At the exclusion of that,
Is refusal of all
Until all is accepted.

Even in judgment,
Then all is judged.
And the One will know.
Rejection.
Though the One is but,
Acceptance

From rejection only,
Judgment may stand,
And She will know,
That which She is not.
Because the desire,
Knowledge from perspective,
And we are,
As we can be,
Therefore we do,
Embrace our judgment.   02/26/10

Notes

You Are

Just as your soul,
Unerringly,
Has guided you,
Though I do not share,
I am not there with you,
Has my soul failed me?
And yet I won't,
From my place I cannot,
Deny you
Your denial of me.
See as you will,
Judge as you must,
For your heart,
I know,
Its guidance true.
To reject who I am,
As celebration of you.
Is for you, to be,
Your cause.   04/15/10

Notes

Don Mateus

Since I first became aware,
You having slid into my conscience,
Riding the waves,
That have been my life,
The uninvited companion.
Laughing at me, not with me, your disdain,
Carelessly disguised,
My ignorance the source,
Of all that amused.
As I drifted, apparently
Seemingly, aimlessly
In the breeze,
Of your contempt,
And yet, and yet
The melancholy veneer,
Carefully crafted by the master,
All the while orchestrated,
At every turn,
Purpose expressed,
The chaos I have been.
And as I balance, on the edge
Prepared now, prepared for,
This appointment with myself,
Your gaze rests with such a,
Curious detachment.
Is it necessary
That I understand?
As I leave the edge
Behind.   07/12/10

Notes

Desperation

I don't think I can tell you
What it is you want to hear,
But I wish that I could share with you
All the loneliness we fear.
Just to be heard
To express and to have felt,
This feeling we carry.
Just once, to be heard,
To not feel swallowed, confined
Shouting from inside.
Plaintive words we've spoken,
Waiting to be heard,
Just once.   06/30/10

Notes

Always Peace

In the choreographed dance,
Some call synchronicity,
The souls of all
Plan, play, and unite.
With ease we accept,
When the dots connect,
The veil of the mystery,
Still its absence reveals.
And the connections,
Are always there.
Conjunction, the magic
The sentient presence,
Is life revealing life,
Though the times,
We stumble through,
As if no meaning,
At all.

Notes

Reflection

We create the reflection
What we see, how we see.
It's not the pond or the mirror or another,
Creating who we are.
This is for us, who we choose to be,
Whether conscious or unconsciously
What we believe, with what we agree.
Presenting ourselves as honesty,
Begins with clarity, with ourselves,
Still yet an aspect,
Complete unto all that we are,
We will arrive once path walked
Only to leave again.
After, not before,
This order since,
Will only follow experience.
Freedom presents,
Living as the light,
Shadows of fear, may retreat
Love as light, truth, and freedom.
Circular, infinite, forever.
Speaking this truth, in time,
Thinking this truth,
Being,
Is never with cost,
Because we discover
We have only given this
To ourselves.   03/27/10

Notes

Remember Me?

The one you have prayed for
The second of two,
From the depths of your suffering,
And still you run.
Of course that from me
You would seek to hide,
But we both know
No escape,
From yourself,
From what it is that follows.
You have come to me,
Answers you deny.
You know I am not afraid,
To give you that you ask.
You have yet to find
In your memory of memories
That our bodies,
The bridge,
Between our reason and heart
Speak to us,
Remind us,
That we would see,
Emotional wreckage
Over how many lifetimes?
Each and everyone
An indication of who we were,
Are becoming.
Each a clue,
To the power lying within.
You will try to run,
You only remember running,
But this time you will not get far,
Your defenses exposed,
That simply cannot,
Blind you more.   4/18/10

Notes

Honestly

The words I hear,
I have heard before.
Each time,
Each word,
Abrasive, corrodes,
Another portion,
Lost.
The contempt
Bearing banner of honesty,
The very insinuation,
Does honesty, no justice.
Leaving that which could,
Champion virtue,
Bastardized in the wake.
Again, this was not
Accurate expression,
Not from where I
Absorb the blow,
Though expression it was.
From each word,
Damage done,
Defending myself,
From your fear.   06/13/10

Notes

Karmic Shuffle

We search and search,
The restless souls
That would occupy,
This frustration.
And upon this pursuit
Of impelling discord,
We emanate
The being,
As ripples, waves,
Endurance dispensed,
Throughout.
We thus affect
And in turn
Are effected,
Unaware, save the day,
We awaken.
Though how
To be fast,
While disguised
From ourselves,
To allow the abandon
Of reckless intent,
Around and through,
Thus being peace,
In the midst of the storm.

05/ 14/ 10

Notes

Authors Note

This Has All Been Said Before, and thank you for getting to this point, is also an expression of myself welcoming the reader to my therapy. Depression has not been my demise rather it has been my salvation. This condition, this gift I have come to understand that I have given to myself, challenged me to have to begin to realize and appreciate, to my own satisfaction, the completely creative and responsible dreamers we human beings are as I relentlessly pursued a recovery on my own terms.

The meaning of life can be absolute or it can be subjective. Both matter and mutually support each other. Life, in every single form matters simply because in the absence of life expressing itself, there is nothing and absolutely, something, anything has to matter more than nothing. Subjectively, the meaning of life is whatever we as an individual attach to it, and it is from this perspective, the singular perspective each and every human provides God, that God has allowed God to come to 'know' God. Just as depression was the gift I, my soul, provided myself, Phil Hammond, as the means through which I would view and explore creation this time, in this space, God has given us to Gods self, to do the same, explore creation on God's behalf.

My learning to recognize and manage depression revealed to me the power of thought and belief and like the double edged sword they will cut both ways. Thought allows a human being to create and manifest their reality, as God intended, and coming to realize that I was the agent of my own misfortune provided the insight and then the strength to use the power of my thought to carve out a path of recovery, confidence and advantage for myself.

Thank you for having shared this with me and perhaps coming closer to your truth for having allowed yourself to witness mine.

About The Author

Phil Hammond is a first time author exploring the topic that has most motivated him for most of his adult life, "What is human consciousness?" Born into 'The Way of Study', (Secret Language of Destiny) the core path in Phil's life has been to choose and identify a principle and then study this principle until he is satisfied with his understanding. Needing to always know, "Why?" it has been his goal in this lifetime to understand who we humans are by dedicating himself to the field of study asking, "Who or what is God, what is God up to if there is a God and what role do humans play in God's creation?" Satisfied that he has achieved his goal, Phil offers, **This Has All Been Said Before**, as testament to his remembering of his truth.

Born in Calgary, Alberta, to Dwayne and Jean Hammond, Phil grew up, actively, in Southern Alberta where he continues to live and play. Graduating from the University of Alberta in 1986 with a Bachelor of Arts, Special Degree, double majoring in economics and political science, Phil has worked a variety of jobs and run several businesses taking him from Edmonton to Montreal, Medicine Hat and Calgary. A self-professed nomad he has been constantly on the move defying and perhaps frustrating those conventional forces in his life while he has followed that voice inside of him, sometimes forced by that voice, to fulfill his destiny. In his own way, Phil feels he has been listening to God and the representatives of Spirit throughout his life, resolving through repetitiveness, practice, awareness, understanding and acceptance those issues in this lifetime, the express purpose of which were to change who he is.

Applying what he has learned from his experience Phil believes that the sharing of his truth will encourage those fellow souls ready for said truths to help themselves in their discovery of who they are. Knowing that we are all here to help each other and in the process fulfill our destiny his ambition is to apply his knowledge in the years to come as a therapist and writer furthering his understanding of consciousness. while allowing others to do the same.

CPSIA information can be obtained at www.ICGtesting.com
228211LV00002B/13/P

9 781456 719661